SHOTS FIRED

SHOTS FIRED

THE FIRST ROUND

BASED ON A TRUE STORY

RICHARD J. DIAZ

Library of Congress Control Number: 2026911074

ISBN: 979-8-9959003-1-3

DISCLAIMER

This book is a work of nonfiction written in the third person. The events described are based on the Author's personal experiences and recollections.

Some names, identifying details, professions, and locations have been changed or combined for privacy and narrative clarity. Any resemblance to persons living or dead, without explicit permission, is coincidental or the result of fictionalization.

The Author has taken care to represent events truthfully; however, certain conversations and interactions may be reconstructed from memory.

This book is dedicated to the loving memory of my parents, John and Marie; to my sisters, Janine and Michelle; to all those whose dedication to service outweighs their own lives; to Jose Mateo, who entrusted me to save his life in the greatest courtroom battle of my own, and to the officers who stood beside him. Finally, to the loving memory of Devin Jaramillo, whose life, regrettably, I could not save.

CONTENTS

PREFACE

What motivated me to write this book was not theory, ideology, or hindsight. It was the look in the eyes of the police officers who sat in that courtroom every day for weeks, supporting their brother-in-arms.

Miami-Dade County deputy sheriffs of the Priority Response Team were present throughout the proceedings, their silence louder than testimony. When our eyes met across the courtroom, I saw it clearly: resolve, hope, anxiety, dependence, and fear.

Fear that I might fail them, and trust that I would not.

I
THE HEIST

The City of Coral Gables is a highly haute municipality established in 1925 that is aptly called "The City Beautiful." Its reputation is well-earned and has endured decades, comparable to Rodeo Drive in West Los Angeles. Located seven miles southwest of Downtown Miami, it is a short drive to Miami International Airport. Looking like a Mediterranean-themed plant community—known for its historic and affluent character and reinforced by its strict zoning, popular landmarks, tourist sites, swanky restaurants, and retail stores—it is home to the nationally known University of Miami.

Its police department boasts the fastest response rate of any police department in the country. Jewelry store heists just don't happen within the city. Period. Well, until it did.

December 5, 2019, 4:12 p.m.

[Prolonged emergency beep signal over the Coral Gables police radio.] "Attention, all units, 25 [alarm] silent hold-up alarm at the Royal Jewelry store, a 325. Miracle Mile."

Lilian Martinez, a lovely seventy-year-old lady and the store's sales representative, took a gunshot wound to her forehead. Although bleeding heavily, she was still conscious—barely holding on, but alert enough to follow basic commands. She sat on the floor with her back propped against the wall, applying pressure to the gaping wound with a towel.

Inside the store, chaos gave way to adrenaline. Eric Emerald, the owner, and Rafael Muina, the manager, moved with notable speed but with zero tactful instinct. The moment the gunman slipped out through the rear door, they armed themselves and chased them with every second captured on the store's indoor and outside security cameras.

Simultaneously, outside, in the store's rear alley, the suspect was scrambling toward the getaway vehicle—a rented U-Haul van. The jewelry store owner raised his weapon and fired several rounds in that direction. The sharp crack of gunfire shattered the air, bullets tearing through the U-Haul's rear windows. One of those rounds found its mark. It struck Ronnie Hall—a forty-one-year-old, six-two, 250-pound muscular ex-robbery convict—in the back, but he didn't go down and instead ran toward the U-Haul van as if unharmed. He was bleeding, desperate, but still moving.

One round fired by the jewelry store owner whizzed across Le Jeune Road and pierced through a glass window at Coral Gables City Hall. It barely missed a city employee named Marco. Fearing an attack that caused chaos at City Hall, the Coral Gables Police Department ordered an immediate shutdown of the entire building and its operations. For a moment, the City believed it was under attack.

[Another prolonged beep.] "Any unit clear for a 3-30 at City Hall?" the dispatcher's voice cut through the static—3-30, code for an active shooter.

Instantly, police radios crackled to life. "Show me en

route," came multiple replies from patrol officers—one after another. Sirens wailed across Coral Gables as all available patrol cars converged on City Hall.

Rick heard them before he saw them. One, then two, then five patrol cars tore past his office, lights flashing against the glass. Whatever was unfolding, it was not routine. He returned to his work, unaware that he would be forced to revisit this moment five years later, when its significance would no longer be abstract.

But within thirty seconds, the tone shifted. "Arrived," the officer said. "Slow down the responding officers. No victims. No blood. No bodies." All officers monitoring the police radio were left asking, *What in the hell is going on?*

The vehicle fled with over a million dollars in jewelry and cash, first speeding north on Le Jeune Road in a white U-Haul van.

Within a minute of the 4:12 p.m. dispatch, a uniformed Coral Gables police officer conducting a traffic stop nearby arrived at the jewelry store. The officer managed to beat the average response time; Coral Gables Fire Rescue was already en route.

Seconds later, he learned what had occurred at the jewelry store just minutes earlier. The incident had been captured on multiple surveillance cameras, both inside and outside the store. The officer identified at least two individuals: a white male who entered the store and committed the robbery, and a second person who drove the getaway vehicle. No further description was immediately available.

The robber was later identified as Hall. He had disguised himself as a United States Postal Service mail carrier, wearing a white mask, white golf gloves, and dark wraparound sunglasses. The disguise was convincing enough for the store owner to buzz him inside. Once through the door, Hall fired a single round that struck Lilian the head. He then emptied the jewelry cases and radioed his accomplice, who had been waiting in a rented U-Haul van in the rear alley, positioned for a quick exit from the alley.

Based on his transmission of the information, the dispatcher shortened it to its main relevance. [After another prolonged beep over the same police emergency radio channel.] "Attention, all units, it's a confirmed 29 [robbery] with a 30 [gunshot] victim..."

"Subject is a white male..."

The paramedics moved quickly, stabilizing Lilian on scene. Her pulse was weak but steady. She needed immediate, emergency medical treatment. Within minutes, she was rushed to Miami's nationally recognized Jackson Memorial Hospital Trauma Center. They could get her there faster by road than waiting for Miami-Dade Police Department's—MDPD's—Air Rescue.

4:16 p.m.

The Coral Gables Police Department received a third 911 call; this one caused yet more confusion. It came from a resident on Mariana Street, just a few blocks north of the jewelry store, close to Le Jeune Road. The resident there had just received a UPS delivery at her house, which had two Ring cameras facing front toward the street. After hearing the UPS driver drop a box off on her porch, she reported seeing two Black males walking up to the UPS truck, each with bags in their hands, climbing inside, apparently with the driver, and the truck then drove away from that location, prompting her to call 911.

But her description did not squarely match the one from

the callers regarding the robber at the jewelry store—a white male. The timing was weird, suspect, and likely coincidental, despite the descriptions of the subjects. *Could there be three subjects instead of two?* Officers were simultaneously confused, astonished, and apoplectic.

The Coral Gables Police Department called security at UPS headquarters and asked if they could assist in locating what now appeared to be a stolen UPS truck with a hostage inside—one of its own employees, Franscico Ortiz. While the UPS truck did not have an interior tracker, Ortiz had one in his pocket linked to UPS' security department. Now, the truck's location, speed, and direction of travel could be monitored, and the robbers were unaware of its existence.

4:25 p.m.

Coral Gables PD issued a countywide notification of what was going on to seek the help of other surrounding police agencies. There were thirty-four municipalities within the county, but the MDPD Communications Bureau had the ability to override all of their communications systems and issue a countywide notification called a "BOLO": "Be on the lookout."

"Be advised—BOLO for an armed robbery. Victim shot in the head. Suspect vehicle last seen northbound on Le Jeune Road. U-Haul van, with the driver's window shot out."

The transmission was clear and tense, the kind of call that for a second or two freezes every police officer. Within seconds, every nearby unit was tuned in, their minds already drawing a mental map—Le Jeune northbound, U-Haul van, shots fired, victim down. Attentive officers were making mental predictions of the next possible routes of travel—an educated guessing game.

4:47 p.m.

"Attention, all units—stand by for update. Officers are now advising the subjects—two Black males—have committed a carjacking. They ditched the U-Haul van and hijacked a UPS truck in the Gables. Both suspects are armed, last seen westbound on Southwest 8th Street and 57th Avenue."

The airwaves went silent, every officer processing the escalation. A robbery, a shooting, now a hijacking. A chase would likely result, and the stakes were now climbing by the second. This scenario had all the makings of a finality that would not end with a voluntary surrender. The greater likelihood was a shoot-out. For the next few minutes, patrol cars sped up and headed to where the UPS truck might be.

II
THE RETURN

Hialeah, Florida, 1975

"Here we are, back in the good ol' USA," Rick's mom said. The words hung in the ninety-eight-degree humid air as the car rolled past the faded pastels and palm tree-lined streets. Home—yet not quite the same—as the Miami they left five years earlier.

Rick was now sixteen. Lean, maybe 150 pounds soaking wet, but highly disciplined. Five years abroad in Spain had shaped him more than he realized—studying at King's College, an international British school where precision and academic excellence mattered, and countless hours in a small dojo dedicated to Okinawan-style karate. Rick had learned three new languages: Spanish, French, and Latin. He'd grown used to order, routine, and respect. He was resilient and highly disciplined.

The house they stood in wasn't theirs—it belonged to the Almeidas, their closest friends who'd opened their doors to the Diaz family of five when they had nowhere else to go.

"We can only stay here for so long," she continued. "They've been good to us, but we can't take advantage of their kindness. You three need to find work and soon—all of you." Her words loomed like a promise and a burden all at once.

She said it with the calm authority of a matriarch—someone who had already made peace with the family's new challenge and struggle. Her tone carried history. She had seen it before—her own mother during the Great Depression, renting out empty rooms in their modest home in Chicago's County Mayo just to keep food on the table. Survival by sacrifice wasn't new to her, nor to the entire family.

"Your mom and I already have jobs," Rick's father added, "but it won't be enough. You kids should first try the fast-food places nearby."

"Nearby" sounded comforting at first, but in reality, it still meant long walks beneath a punishing South Florida sun, which the family had lost memory of due to the dry heat of Madrid in the summer and the collaboration of its icy, dry, cold, and windy winters. They now remembered that Miami's heat was unique, the type that stuck to your skin: humidity that made every breath feel heavy, and the inevitability of afternoon storms that rolled in like clockwork.

There was sadness, but no bitterness, in the Almeida house that night; hope and apprehension lingered, but it would soon yield to quiet determination. A stark reality had now set in—and fast. They were starting over, one uncertain step at a time, finding refuge, however temporarily fragile, now, in the Almeidas' Hialeah home.

The next morning, the three siblings fanned out, walking from one nearby fast-food restaurant to the next under the relentless steamy summer heat. One sister quickly landed a job at McDonald's; the other sister found work at one of the three Burger Kings scattered across the city that same afternoon.

Rick—the only boy—wasn't so fortunate. Several job

applications later, not a single bite, and Rick was feeling the pressure. His continued unemployment was not an option. A few more days passed—nothing. Intuition told him to go back to the first one that had turned him down, a thin hope that luck would strike this time.

It was the Burger King where the manager, Mario Diez, only days earlier had looked him in the eye and smiled warmly, while also disappointingly turning Rick away. This visit, he handed Rick a meal instead of a rejection slip.

"Here's a Whopper, large fries, and a Coke, kid," Mario said, sliding the tray across the front counter. "But we still have no opening. Don't worry, keep applying; there are many fast-food places around here. You'll find something sooner or later."

"I don't have a later, sir. I need a job—not tomorrow, I need one now," Rick answered, his voice caught somewhere between imploring and begging.

"Sounds like you've got a good head on your shoulders. You're sixteen, right? Already finished high school so young and about to start college?"

"Yes, sir."

"Miami-Dade Community College, I take it?"

"Yes, sir."

Mario raised an eyebrow, a grin tugging at the corner of his mouth. "What's with your military tone? 'Yes, sir'; 'No, sir.' You sound like you're reporting for duty."

Rick smiled. "I was hoping that I was." Even at sixteen years old, he had a quick, witty sense of humor. "My dad was in the Army. And I've been in martial arts since I was ten." He was all so humbly proud—quite mature, confident, and very hungry—not for a free burger, but for a chance at a job.

The manager paused and scratched his chin, studying Rick for a moment before scribbling something on a napkin.

"Young man, call this number from time to time. It rings straight to my office. Maybe you'll get lucky, and a spot opens up. It might only be part-time, and we only pay minimum wage. No tips here either."

Rick chuckled softly. "Sir, right now I make less than that."

Mario laughed, shaking his head. "Ah, so you're a comedian, too." He glanced toward the kitchen, where the sounds of the plastic orange clattering trays and sizzling burgers on the retching grill were picking up. The customer line was swelling.

"All right, I've got to get back. It looks like the breakfast rush is about to hit. Keep that number, kid. You never know when a spot might open."

"Can I call every day?" Rick asked.

Mario's cold laugh quickly turned to a warm smile, "Yes, of course, even twice—like I said, you never know."

Rick nodded and tucked the napkin deep into his pocket. He slid into a corner booth and unwrapped the Whopper, the irresistible smell of grilled beef covered by a slice of melted American cheese pressed by ketchup, four chip pickles, lettuce, two tomato slices, and mayonnaise all filling the air in front of him. He hadn't eaten a Burger King burger in years.

The first bite hit hard—a warm sesame-seed bun, smoky beef patty, and quite real. The fresh fries weren't quite as good as McDonald's, but they did the job, and the Coke—ice-cold and fizzy—washed it all down like a small reward after a long, humid day filled with rejection.

For a few quiet minutes, despite the disappointment, it felt good just to sit there, staring a gaze, to taste something that didn't feel borrowed or uncertain. Then he crumpled the waxy wrapper, stood up, and brushed the crumbs from his hands. Before leaving, he entered the men's bathroom to wash his hands.

Time to keep looking—hunting, actually...

Walking outside the dining room and through the parking lot, Rick couldn't help but notice discarded Burger King paraphernalia wrappers, french fry boxes, greasy bags, and empty waxed soda cups, their lids and straws caught in the breeze while the Styrofoam coffee cups rolled aimlessly. Cigarette butts abounded along the ground, where rubbish was trapped in the cracked asphalt. The "landscaping"—if one could even call it that—was a patchwork of dry soil and dead plants, more tumbleweed than greenery.

He started at the entrance of the parking lot and worked his way around to the exit, picking up all of the trash into a discarded bag and throwing it away in the rear dumpster. It took about an hour, but the parking lot was now noticeably litter-free; perhaps most people wouldn't have noticed. But Rick did.

People like him always did.

Having worked up a good sweat, Rick went back inside the Burger King, waiting for the lunch rush to subside to show off his work to Mario. He headed straight for the water fountain, leaning down to take a long, cold drink—just enough to wash the dryness from his throat. Then he pushed open the men's restroom door and turned on the faucet, letting the cool stream run over his head. The water soaked through his hair, along his overheated scalp, dripping down the back of his neck and around his warm, beet-red face. The cool relief was instant and pleasantly transforming. He could feel his body temperature drop, the heat leaving him in slow waves.

While staring into the mirror, thinking about how he'd show his grit to the manager, the door unexpectedly swung open, and Mario nearly collided with him. Rick's hair was still dripping wet, and his face still flushed.

"What happened to you? I thought you'd left," Mario said, spotting Rick by the sink, water droplets still falling from his hair down his face as he reached for a paper towel.

Rick straightened up, wiping his face with a sheet of coarse paper towel. "Thought I'd show you what I can do," he said, nodding toward the door. "Please take a minute to look at the parking lot."

Mario raised an eyebrow. "At what? The parking lot?"

"Yes, sir," Rick said simply.

Mario stared at him for a moment, then chuckled under his breath. "All right, kid," he said, "Let's go see."

Rick wasn't sure if Mario's use of the word "kid" was endearing, or an expression of his bothersome reaction to Rick's pressure.

They stepped outside. A moment of opportunity for Rick. Anxiety and anticipation now substituted to his overheated body temperature.

Mario's eyes scanned the back of the parking lot. He paced further, turned a full circle, studying the more distant area, and his jaw progressively dropped, leaving a look of disbelief on his face. He turned to Rick but said nothing, as if searching for the right words.

"Oh, and sir, the men's room needs toilet paper and the aromatizer isn't working. It's not broken; it just has a dead battery."

"May I ask, how do you know that?"

Rick shrugged, knowing the explanation could be the make-or-break point..."Well, sir, I went into the ladies' room—announcing myself of course—took the battery from that unit, tested it in the men's, and then put it back in the ladies' side. Voilà—which told me it was the battery all along."

Mario paused and stared into the distance for a second or two, then shook his head with a grin. "All right, kid.

You've got a job. I'll have to let someone go—and I think I know who it will be. Be here tomorrow morning. Full-time spot. We open at ten, but setup starts at eight. Don't be late."

Rick was exhilarated. "Yes, sir!" he said, trying to keep his composure but unable to hide the grin stretching across his face.

"You have a ride?"

Rick shook his head. "Doubt it, sir. It's less than an hour's walk, but maybe I can get a ride. Either way, I'll be here."

Mario nodded. "That's what I like to hear."

Rick had never been a no-show or a sick-callout, and it wasn't going to start now. He extended his hand. "Thank you, sir."

Mario took it, holding Rick's gaze for a moment. There was pride in Rick's eyes—not showy, but the kind that came from recognizing a victory.

For his part, Mario seemed relieved. He knew he was doing right, but he also knew he was acquiring a solid, mature new hire whom he could rely on.

"I myself came here from Cuba as a teenager. I know what that change feels like—not easy," Mario said. "And I know how exciting it is to get your first job. See you *mañana*."

"Yes, sir," Rick said with a grin of accomplishment and commitment as he walked away with an obvious bouncing pep in his step.

From day one, Rick's learning curve pushed him from one station to the next: fries, broiler, drinks, shakes, and making his first burger to "the board." Then he graduated to the crown-prize: order-taking and order-pickup. No one could compete with his speed and accuracy. He won first place in a contest as to who could make the quickest

Whopper while following the specific amount of each additive and order of assembly; his record was seven seconds.

On his seventeenth birthday, Rick asked his mother to go with him to the local Armed Forces recruitment office just down the street from the same BK. He had made up his mind—he was leaving Burger King behind and joining the Air Force to become a fighter pilot. Even though he was a minor, with parental consent at seventeen, he could legally join. Rick sensed his mother's disapproval. After all, the Vietnam War death toll was a reflective memory of the conflict that raged up until 1975—only two years earlier.

He passed the written test, medical exam, fitness requirements, and background check. His final step was a month or so later. It was an interview at the Koger Center in Doral, Florida, where he would be sworn in and receive his report date for boot camp.

The complex was massive, housing numerous federal agencies—DEA, Secret Service, and others. Just driving through and walking into the Armed Forces building gave Rick a profound sense of the strength and authority of the US government. Rick had sailed through the selection process, and the interview went fast and smooth. Armed Services Recruiting was a top priority of the Carter administration.

Not long after his interview, Rick was called to get sworn in, after which, within a few days or short weeks, he'd be shipped out for his basic training. The last steps included job selection and taking an oath on a Bible.

"You say you want to fly military combat jets?"

"Yes, sir," Rick replied. "An F-4 Phantom."

"Well, that isn't happening. You're mildly colorblind. Were you not aware of that? I'm sorry." He didn't pause long enough for the apology to land on Rick. "You still have a few good options—military police, firefighter, or cook."

Rick's facial expression needed no words. But he needed to explain why he was now having regrets. "I am already a cook, and if I wanted to be a cop or fireman, I'd do it here, not in the military. I wanted to be a pilot."

"Look," the uniformed man continued, lowering his voice, "I could catch hell for saying this—but don't walk through that door on the other side. In that room are four things: a staff sergeant, a US flag, a Bible, and a *really* loud fan. Once they swear you in, the US Air Force owns you." He gestured behind Rick. "Go back the way you came. And hurry."

Rick nodded, turned toward the door, and left the building as discreetly as he could. *Back to Burger King*, he thought.

Not long thereafter, Rick was sent to Burger King University (BKU), a management school in Miami, and then promoted by Mario to assistant manager at the same BK.

One year later, Mario sadly passed. The franchise owner, Ms. Carol Sharpe, made Rick, then only seventeen years old, the store manager.

Rick's ascent was not happenstance; it was destiny. But he knew that working at a franchise-owned store—one of three in Hialeah—the best he could hope for was to become the regional manager over all stores.

He immediately made several changes—some that he learned at BKU but that were still rejected by Mario at first, just tightening up what needed fixing. Yet, one of those changes would redirect Rick's life in a way he could never have imagined. It was the seed that Rick planted that would give life to his main diversion from then on. No more giving police officers a 50 percent discount on their meals. They would pay nothing. Free meals for on-duty, uniformed patrol police officers. His reasoning was simple: public safety.

For one, the competition among the neighboring fast-food restaurants was fierce. Second, at the time, there were rival gangs in South Florida, from Hialeah to Carol City, and others rooted deep within the inner city of Miami.

The Jamaican Posse made the city's streets tense, territorial, and often outright deadly. Cocaine was becoming boomingly popular; contraband marijuana trafficking was at an all-time high. And control over the street sale of narcotics was a big part of the violent activities among the gangster-like groups.

It was common for their members to "meet and eat" at local fast-food restaurants, such as this particular Burger King franchise in the heart of West Hialeah.

Their loud, intimidating presence in the restaurant had a way of changing the atmosphere the moment they walked in. Customers grew uneasy, conversations faded, and the air took on a quiet tension. They were easy to spot, swaggering in with cocky confidence that bordered on menace.

They all drove fast and flashy cars—Camaro Z28s, Firebird Trans Ams, and Corvette L82s: all polished to perfection, most of them customized to stand out even more. The members were generally bulked up, muscles pumped and stretched from steroids, their shirts fitting like warnings. A few were real fighters—none more infamous than Karate Ray. By his nickname, Rick knew he must have been at an advanced degree, but Rick was at a small, discreet dojo that did not compete against any school, and for good reason. Gōjū-ryū students were drilled in keeping their skills to themselves.

When Karate Ray came into Rick's Burger King, the air thickened. Their stare downs were electric, the kind that made everyone else look away. His sensei, Ruben, taught Rick old-school, like Master Po trained Little Grasshopper in the then-famed *Kung Fu* series. As unassuming as lethal. If they faced off, no one in that restaurant would forget it.

Whereas Rick was a lean, agile, and quick fighter, Karate Ray was the polar opposite: a 200-pounder of solid, shredded muscle.

When Rick first returned to Miami in 1975, he wanted to join a local school. He couldn't afford the dues, but he still opened the Yellow Pages and jotted down every karate school in Miami. He visited all of them. He found one—a very special and old school—Ruben Font's Gōjūī-ryū dojo in a rough part of town. The windows were purposely covered by shade blinds so nobody could watch the training from outside. No guests allowed either. Invitation granted only upon apparent demonstrated interest. And even then, only for a few minutes.

It was like no other, and Ruben took an immediate interest in Rick, as he had heard of Fabian, Rick's sensei from the Madrid dojo. He welcomed Rick to do one *kata*-and-spar for one minute of *kumite* with one of Ruben's green-belted students.

Ruben said, "You are welcome to learn here. It's called 'The Way.'"

But Rick could not pay the first month's dues: $15. Around his neck, Rick always wore an 18-karat gold chain—a gift from his father.

"You can use that chain to pay, you know," Ruben said.

Rick didn't hesitate. He unclasped it and handed it over.

"I wanted to see if you actually meant it," Ruben said. "Now I know. I will hold onto it. If you make your dues on time, I will return it."

Over the years, Rick trained at the school. His schedule

cut into sessions more often than he liked, but he pushed through. He earned a brown belt—not the coveted black, but close enough to show he'd put in real work—enough to handle any gang member he might, one day, have to confront.

After a few months of paying on time, the old instructor smiled, headed to his office in the dojo, reached into his desk drawer, pulled out the same gold chain, and handed it to Rick with a deep bow.

Ruben was as old-school as they came. Once he knew that Rick was a serious student, and despite his frequent schedule conflicts, every Saturday morning, he trained Rick one-on-one in his home garage. The space was tidy—mats rolled to one side, shuriken weapons, a katana sword lined up along the wall, and a faint smell of sweat and oil hanging in the air.

Ruben was a master of jiujitsu, aikido, judo, and kung fu. He studied under Gōsei Yamagochi, the son of Gōjū-ryū founder—Gōgen Yamagochi—nicknamed "The Cat." Ruben taught Rick everything he knew—not just how to fight, but how to command control in any space he entered outside of combat.

Rick became like a prodigal son to Ruben. He'd return to the dojo for periods and then disappear for years at a time. On every return, Ruben stripped Rick of his colored belt and tossed him a brand-new white one—a hard, but necessary lesson, not only for Rick, but for the other dojo students as well.

Every time, Ruben reminded Rick that he had lost "The Way." No one received special treatment. Commitment mattered. Those who devoted themselves to their consistent, routine training earned their rank; absence erased it. Ruben knew that Rick's "sabbaticals" were not from disinterest but rather governed by his heavy work-school schedule. Saturday lessons alone were insufficient. At least three days a week were required to stay in the dojo—or you were gone. After twenty years of these "on-and-offs," Ruben unexpectedly tested Rick and handed him a black belt.

One day, Ms. Sharpe brought in her nephew, Paul. Instead of working his way up like everyone else, Paul was instantly handed the title of assistant manager and assigned to Rick. His job wasn't to be shadowed—it was to teach Paul everything he knew. Rick saw the writing on the wall.

He did the quick math on the free meals for cops. At the time, an off-duty uniformed officer charged about $17 an hour. A Whopper, fries, and a Coke ran the restaurant roughly $2.50. On average, an officer would sit in the dining room for about half an hour while eating—a small investment in security.

Within a few short weeks, whether morning, afternoon, or evening, you could drive past the restaurant and almost always see a marked police car parked out front. The presence of law enforcement now nearly doubled, and the once-frequent 911 calls over "gang issues" at this BK faded into memory.

Carol Sharpe took notice. By the end of 1978, the store's annual sales had rocketed from $650,000 to nearly a million dollars. Rick's initiative hadn't just brought safety—it brought profit. Soon after, he was promoted to Hialeah regional manager, overseeing all three city locations. Unsurprisingly, Paul was now promoted to manager.

By then, in 1977, Rick knew his days at BK were numbered. He needed a new career path.

Ms. Sharpe often said she had "big plans for Rick," but fate had plans of its own—and one unforeseen moment would spark Rick's next move, one entirely his own. Would it be coincidence, happenstance, or destiny?

Hialeah Gardens bordered the city of Hialeah to the

west. The city covered less than four square miles—mostly industrial—and was patrolled by a very small police department, maybe ten to fifteen officers in total, including supervisors and the chief.

Hialeah Gardens Police Chief Keith Joy was a familiar face at Rick's Burger King—one of those regulars who needed no introduction. One afternoon, while placing his usual order at the BK, the chief casually extended Rick an invitation: a ride-along as a civilian observer.

Rick had never heard of such a thing before, but the idea grabbed him instantly. The chance to ride in a patrol car, see the city streets through a cop's eyes—it was irresistible. To him, it felt like being handed a golden ticket to Disney World—only better, because this thrill didn't require a long drive or a price of admission.

"Let's do a Friday afternoon shift, because that's usually when good shit goes down," Keith said. "Good shit?"

Rick muttered under his breath, eyebrows knitting together. What did he mean by that?

The next Friday, Rick did the ride-along as a "civilian observer." They sat in a marked Hialeah Gardens cruiser in the station's lot. It was 5:00 p.m.

Keith turned to Rick with that half-smirk officers used when they were about to test you. "You know how to use a shotgun?"

Rick had never touched a firearm of any kind, much less a pump shotgun.

Before he could respond, Chief Joy cut in with the kind of calm authority that made you stop thinking and start listening. "Okay. Let me show you."

They climbed out of the patrol car together. Keith popped the trunk. On a rack lay a Remington 870, its wood stock worn smoothly by use and hands. Up close, it looked less like something from a movie and more like a simplified tool, but it was heavy, honest, and deliberate. He pressed a release to unlatch the weapon and pulled it out with relaxed confidence.

Rick listened, watched, and studied the handling. The lesson was short and precise, the kind you remembered because it left no room for misunderstanding. It had a certain look, sound, and feel: *click-click*.

"One shell is already in the chamber and four more in the magazine," Keith said, voice matter-of-fact.

Rick felt the hair at the back of his neck prick—not in panic, but out of respect for the power he now carried. This was not a toy, but rather something that demanded attention and discipline.

Keith laid a finger along the stock and nodded. "That's the safety there. This is a pump gun—you cycle the action back first, then forward to chamber a round. After you fire, you'll cycle it again to load the next cartridge. It's not automatic—it's manual. The sling holds five extra cartridges. Hopefully, you won't need it, but let me show you."

He emptied the shotgun, the round in the chamber, and those in the magazine. He did it with remarkable speed. "Now, hold it in your hands and rack one into the chamber." It was unusually symbolic and intimidating as it was lethal.

Rick could feel his heart race. He was in very unfamiliar territory—a bit uncomfortable, and now he was about to take a ride where he *might* have to use a shotgun.

"Also, it has a kick," Keith said, adjusting the shotgun firmly against—and into—Rick's shoulder and armpit. "You gotta put your body into it to absorb the recoil and control the discharge—it has a kick." He bent slightly forward and assumed a shoulder-width stance.

Rick mirrored him.

"Aim at the middle of the body. We call it center of mass, but if you miss high and blow off the head, don't worry. Just be close to the target and make sure I am not!"

It was all so immediate and overwhelming, but backing out wasn't an option. "Thanks, but no thanks" was not in Rick's vocabulary on a challenge like this one. There was no backing out now. This was a new reality that was a part of the Uniform Patrol mission.

They secured the shotgun back in the trunk and climbed back into the patrol car. "Let's roll," Keith said, flipping the ignition. He advised Dispatch that he was in service with "a civilian observer." It was now almost six o'clock.

"I picked the six-to-two shift," Keith added, glancing over his clipboard notes as he adjusted the rear and driver's side-view mirrors, "cause that's when shit happens."

Rick had heard those exact words before—just a week earlier, from Keith at the BK. He now knew exactly what he meant.

The sun was setting, and it was getting dark quickly on this cool winter night. As they were driving through Hialeah Gardens, the radio was quiet. A light fog was settling in. Traffic was light. It all seemed mundane, yet a little eerie.

Keith said, "We use our senses, primarily our eyes, and we tone our ears to the surroundings and the police radio. It's an art."

Keith suddenly reached down and flipped a toggle switch Rick didn't recognize, but it illuminated the overhead blue rotating lights. He then hit another switch, and the siren chirped. They rolled up behind a car approaching an intersection. Nothing seemed off.

Rick had not seen the car commit any moving violation. *What is going on?* he wondered.

Then Keith hit another switch, and the patrol car's siren chirped twice. The driver in the car ahead immediately tapped its brakes, turned on their indicator, and pulled into a nearby parking lot. Rick had no idea what was going on or why this traffic stop was happening. Nothing seemed out of the ordinary. It was now pitch-black—a moonless night, adding to the mystery.

Keith immediately opened the door on his side, which Rick found odd because he didn't immediately get out. Rather, he was sitting on only half of the seat. That seemed even more unusual, but surely Rick would get an explanation later.

As his eyes stayed fixed on the vehicle in front of them, Keith spoke through the radio. "Dispatch, this is Unit 1. Show me on a 19"—a number that meant a traffic stop—"behind a vehicle. Tag Alpha November Romeo Eight Delta Nine [ANR 8D9]. Vehicle is a white Chevy Impala, four-door, dark-tinted windows, unknown number of occupants." Between the film and the darkness of the night, it was impossible to tell.

"'Nineteen is a traffic stop, kid."

The dispatcher responded immediately, "QSL, Unit 1"—police code for "roger that." "Do you need a 15?"

Rick caught that one. *Backup.* His pulse quickened a little.

"Negative, QRU for now," Keith answered.

"QRU?" Rick whispered to himself.

"QRU means 'I'm good.' No backup needed yet," Keith replied. He quickly asked, "Rick, where are we?"

"One-oh-third Street, sir," Rick responded.

"Negative," Keith said, eyes on the road. He keyed the

police radio microphone. "We're westbound on Northwest 103, just east of the Palmetto." He turned to Rick. "That's how you describe it. That detail can save your life—actually, *both* of ours."

Rick muttered to himself, *"Okay, that seemed strange..."* He thought about it for a moment, then let it go. Later, he rethought the correction, and it made sense.

Up until now, the night and its surroundings have been uncomfortably quiet and lonesome. An occasional vehicle would pass by, slowing down out of curiosity. Keith watched everything in his periphery but kept his eyes fixed on the stopped Impala.

"Kid," he said, low and direct, "if some shit goes down, you get on the radio and say, 'Unit 1 needs a 315.'"

Rick let the words sit for a second.

"That's code for an officer needs emergency help. Got it? Dispatch already knows exactly where we are."

"And then what?" Rick asked.

Keith shrugged a fraction, the kind of shrug that carried experience. "We don't have a manual or precise policy for that, my boy. Nobody can train for every possible scenario. If they could, you'd never graduate. You're not an officer, but if you were, you'd have to react one way. As a civilian, the rules are different. So, if any shit does go down, forget about me, get the shotgun to protect yourself. Then get on the radio and answer the dispatcher's questions.

Rick wondered if this was melodrama or reality. "Anything else?" he asked.

"Nope." Keith's tone tightened. "I'll approach the driver's side. You stay in the car, or if you prefer, you can walk up with me to the car—if so, just stay behind me. This is a routine traffic stop for a nonmoving violation. If the driver's paperwork is in order, has no warrants, and he—or she—is courteous, I will send them on their way. If I get an attitude, the driver gets a ticket. Plain and simple."

A lesson Rick took from that conversation as a civilian—and never forgotten—was simple: Always be courteous to any officer who pulls you over, even if you're in the wrong. Show respect, and maybe you catch a break. Don't do anything that could make the officer feel fear or threatened. Act like an asshole, and you're guaranteed a ticket—or worse, an arrest.

Rick wasn't about to lie back and sit in the passenger seat. "Chief, I'm following you." Was he afraid of being alone in the car and taking the path of lesser fear? Or was this a streak of bravado, a need to prove himself? Only he knew—and less than a year later, the world would.

As they approached, Rick's heart began to pound as if it might burst from his chest. The night was now total darkness. Heat crept up his body, and his breathing grew heavier. Between the uncertainty and the anxiety, there was fear—but, strangely, a flicker of excitement, too, a thrill that made it almost...fun.

But what really fell ever so strongly on Rick was the sense of power and control behind the combination of those feelings. It was a rush that could not be accurately described by even the greatest writer. It can only be known to those who have actually sat there in uniform, bearing the weight of public safety with nothing but their training, a badge, and a six-shot revolver.

As soon as Keith got fully out of the patrol car, he unsnapped his right-side holster, making his sidearm more retrievable, even if by only a millisecond. That single movement told Rick everything he needed to know at the time: Even a "routine" traffic stop carried danger waiting behind it.

Keith then swung the spotlight on his unit's left pillar, catching the driver's side mirror in its beam and blinding whoever was behind the wheel.

Smart move, Rick thought. This was not melodrama, yet it seemed so surreal.

Keith then flipped on what looked like a two-foot-long, battery-powered flashlight. He carried it in his left hand, sweeping it across the driver's window and occasionally over the rear and side windows. Every movement had been trained, practiced, and was now in synchronized execution. Slow and decisive, all senses alive and alert—pure survival tactics.

Rick followed Keith as he walked up slowly to the rear of the vehicle and felt the trunk to confirm it was closed. He stayed safely behind the rear door and kept his body hugged to the side of the civilian vehicle as he moved forward.

"Good evening. I'm an officer with the Hialeah Gardens Police. Please roll down all the windows. How many people are in the car?"

"Only me," the driver said.

As the windows slowly rolled down, the silhouette of a female driver came into view. Both of her hands were on the steering wheel.

Rick felt some relief when she advised Keith that she was an off-duty police officer on her way to visit her ailing mother, who lived nearby. Once her identity and purpose were confirmed, any remaining fear and anxiety dissipated.

As a mere courtesy, Keith pointed out the overdue decal on her license plate. The woman asked if she could take a look.

"Absolutely," Keith replied.

She stepped out of the car and walked to the rear, hands

on her hips as she stared at the spot where the decal should've been. "Shit," she muttered. "I just renewed it. The sticker must've been stolen; those things don't just fall off."

She returned to her car, dug into its glove box, and pulled out her current registration; it had, in fact, just been issued. She flipped it over, and there it was: the new decal, still stapled to the back of the registration. A wave of relief washed over her as she tinged with some embarrassment.

"Shit happens," Keith laughed, a small grin spreading across his face. "Well, look at that. I was wrong, and so were you. I thought I had a nonmoving traffic violation, and you thought your decal was stolen."

They exchanged a few collegiate pleasantries before Keith shut off the overhead lights on his unit.

"Stay safe," he said. "I hope your mom gets better."

"You stay safe as well." She paused, then added, "By the way, you said you were an officer—but that gold badge says *Chief*."

Keith chuckled. "I didn't want to intimidate you."

She shot back without missing a beat. "Well, I hate to burst your bubble, but you *did*—even being an officer myself."

They both recognized it then—the unspoken bond between two officers, immediate, rare, but special. This was a brother-sister bond profession. Rick was only beginning to see it, but even to him, it felt unmistakably special. Rick didn't have that camaraderie at BK, and he wasn't going to live it in the military.

Keith began walking toward the unit, Rick close behind. Once in the car, Keith said, "See, Rick, just because we're cops doesn't mean we're always right. Things aren't always what they first appear."

What struck Rick wasn't the truth of those words—it was

how this traffic stop, routine and harmless in the end, could have turned deadly in an instant. He smirked and somewhat snarkily said, "So that's what you meant when you said the 'good shit' happens on the afternoon shift?"

Keith smirked back. "Relax, kid. The night's still young. And Hialeah is our neighbor. That's a very busy patrol, and if we are asked to back them up, that's automatic jurisdiction. Kinda neat!"

They climbed into the car and started the engine, the low rumble filling the quiet night. Rick let the silence stretch just long enough before asking, "Keith, what are the requirements to be a police officer?"

Keith laughed. "You know, Rick, I think you have them all, and more. We've actually got an opening, and a new academy class starts in a few months. It will take about five to six months to finish. You won't have any problem making it. You could have a great law enforcement career. You've got good instincts, you have the academics, multiple languages—I've seen your work ethic and leadership at BK. You control your fear. You'd climb the ranks fast."

They stopped at a red light, the patrol car idling quietly.

Keith glanced at him, noting Rick's attentive posture. He paused, choosing his words carefully. "But let me be honest with you...Hialeah Gardens PD is way too small for a candidate like you."

Rick listened, every word sinking in.

"Sure, I could hire you," Keith continued, tone shifting, "but this place is as political as it gets. You'd love being a cop, but you'd hate working here."

Rick nodded, absorbing the words that sounded like an invitation but with caution.

"Apply with the county," Keith advised. "It's actually called the Public Safety Department—PSD. That's the way to go. One of the best public departments in the country—definitely the best in the state. If that doesn't work out, call me...but don't wait too long. Our mayor is up for reelection, and if she loses, I'm out."

"And then what?" Rick asked, brow furrowed.

"Well, shit," Keith said with a smirk, "I'll apply to PSD, too!"

Rick studied him for a moment, then asked, "But wouldn't you have to start over—as an officer, not a supervisor?"

"Yup," Keith answered, unapologetically, matter-of-fact. Then he tapped a finger against his chest. "Listen, the measure of a good cop—a real cop—has nothing to do with the chevron stripes on your sleeves or the bars or stars on your collar. It's what drives you to do what's right. That's it."

Keith needn't have said anymore. The message was clear and stuck hard. "I love being *El Jefe*, but I'd have no problem going back as a silver-badged road patrol officer, here or with the county."

He leaned back in his seat and added, "Once you're in the academy, you're in. If the county doesn't take you or isn't hiring, try the other good South Florida departments—Coral Gables, for example. Then you can move around. Get the FDLE [Florida Department of Law Enforcement] certificate. That's your ticket."

"Any others?" Rick asked.

Keith let the question hang, eyes scanning the street. After a long pause, he shrugged. "Ah...I really can't think of any. Apply to the county. You'll get in. You're exactly what they're looking for. You've never been arrested, right?"

Rick jerked back, surprised.

Keith smirked. "I'm just kidding—I already ran you through our criminal justice database."

"You did?" Rick asked.

"Remember what I told you two minutes ago? Things aren't always what they seem. You think I was going to put a 'friendly stranger' in my patrol car without some checking? Come on."

He leaned in a little toward Rick. Although nobody was anywhere near to listen, this seemed like an important message, his tone sharpening. "If you want to survive as a good cop, remember this: Assume *everyone* is untrustworthy until they prove you wrong. And even then, some of the ones you think you can trust will still disappoint you later. But that's just life." He then retracted, but his gaze remained profound and meaningful.

That was bitter cold advice—something Rick had never heard, not even from his father. In that moment, he realized Keith was not just a small-town mayor's political appointee; his sage wisdom ran deeper than the five gold stars pinned to each side of his uniform shirt collars.

"And remember this: A cop never gets wet, never goes hungry, and always goes home after the shift," Keith said.

The next morning, Rick drove straight to the PSD headquarters building and filled out an application for police officer. They were hiring! It felt so thrillingly strange—foreign, almost—but all so right, too.

The application was several pages long, but Rick came prepared. The clerk was astonished when he completed every blank and had brought along with him copies of everything he thought he'd be asked for.

"Impressive," she said.

Rick smiled back.

"How bad do you want to wear the silver badge?" she asked.

"Bad enough," Rick retorted.

"Good luck to you Richard," she said as she put the papers into an envelope.

III
THE OFF-DUTY DECISION

Late November 2019

[Jose Mateo on the phone with his friend, Ryan Lindner.] "Hey, buddy, what's up?"

"All good. Listen—they're looking for some off-duties at Aventura Mall for the next six weeks. We can make a ton of OT."

"I'm in. You?"

"Yeah, dude. What are we doing?"

"Simple gig. Cruise the parking lots. Mostly deterrence. They've had a few 26s [vehicle break-ins], 34s [fights], an occasional 27 [shoplifter]."

"Sounds good to me."

"I'm pulling doubles on my days off. The PRT training this week was grueling."

"Count me in."

"All right, then. We start tomorrow at 2:00 p.m. See you there."

A week later, on December 5, 2019, they each showed up in their separate units and did slow patrols through the parking lots of Aventura. Their assignments included occasionally stationing themselves in front of the walkway entrances and strolling a bit on foot throughout the mall walkways. Visibility and deterrence were behind their assignment.

4:53 p.m.

[Radio static.] "Attention, all units, countywide BOLO reference the 29 and 330 in the Gables. Two subjects hijacked a UPS truck and took the driver hostage. They are westbound on Southwest 8th Street from 57th Avenue."

"They got balls, dude. An armed robbery in the Gables, shots fired at an employee, and now this?"

Mateo leaned forward, eyes fixed on the chaos ahead. "What do you think?" he asked, voice low, steady.

Lindner squinted through the windshield, pulse quickening. "Dude, they are far away; we are talking a good twenty to twenty-five miles. We can maybe intersect if they go north, but south or west...with this traffic..." He was not optimistic.

"It's a freaking UPS truck, not a V8 Vette," Mateo reassured. "I think they'll hit 826, maybe the Turnpike, north or south, who knows?"

"Well?" Lindner asked.

"Fuck it, bro. Let's go."

"North or south?" asked Lindner.

"Let's do south..." considered Mateo. "No, let's go north instead. I'm feeling lucky today. We have a better chance of catching them if they go north. It's fifty-fifty, so go north."

"Okay. Let me grab my gear from the unit and we'll double up—or you want to ride with me?" Lindner called out, leaning from his window toward Mateo's car. Both engines idled, exhaust drifting between them.

"You've got one preventable accident on your record.

I've got none. You can't afford a second one—I can afford a first. I'm driving," Mateo shot back. "Light us up and move it. Dispatch says they're on the Turnpike, northbound. The county's listening, but no one's actually on them yet. I was right: They're northbound."

Lindner quickly climbed out of his unit, shaking his head. "We will catch some shit for ditching the off-duty post."

Mateo shrugged. "So what? We are PRT. We got this..."

"Yeah, we won't get the extra-duty pay and might get banned from that mall, but fleeing armed robbers with a hostage versus a possible shoplifter? No-brainer. There's a bunch of off-duties all over this time of year. Let's roll, man!"

"I'm hurrying! Relax!" Lindner slammed his trunk. In seconds, he was in Mateo's unit, the front passenger door slamming behind him.

"How fast can a UPS truck move?" Mateo asked.

"Beats me. Light it up," Lindner said.

Each officer activated their body-worn cameras [BWCs], which only captured what the lens happened to see, as it sat about twelve inches below an officer's actual line of sight.

Mateo's overhead lights illuminated, and the siren wailed to life, slicing through the holiday chaos in the mall's parking lot. Getting out of it was a nightmare. Christmas shoppers clogged every lane, horns blaring, pedestrians carrying shopping bags and weaving between cars.

They threaded themselves around parked and moving cars as they arrowed out of the mall.

"Careful, dude!" Lindner yelled, gripping the dashboard.

Mateo didn't flinch. His foot stayed heavy on the gas, the engine howling in protest as the cruiser shot onto the main road. The cruiser had factory-installed reinforcements, but none were built for continual punishment—reinforced brakes, stiffened struts, a steel push bar—but it lacked the muscle of a true interceptor. No turbo. Just determination and steel on wheels.

When they finally broke free onto the open road, the adrenaline began to pump faster. Tires screeched as they headed westbound, generally toward Florida's Turnpike, coming from the far eastern part of the county. The mild traffic allowed them to comfortably maintain a high speed. Luck was also on their side, as every light was green or yellow.

The road conditions were good, with full traction and clear visibility. It hadn't rained in days. None of that mattered at over 100 miles per hour. With civilian cars cruising at sixty, threading the needle through slower traffic was still a high-risk maneuver.

Radio traffic fell silent. In moments like this, the airwaves stayed clear unless critical information broke through—unless another crisis ignited at the same time. Several units were already en route to the tracking location, but none had visual contact with the UPS truck *yet*.

Time was slipping away *fast*.

It was always the same when a marked unit came up behind them with lights and siren: some drivers steered left, others right, while some panic-braked in the middle of the lane. Instinct became the officer's only reliable predictor—reading civilian drivers' movements before they happened.

"Remember, they're in a UPS truck," Mateo said. "I figure that rig can maybe do sixty on a straight. Do the triangulation math, Mateo—assuming they stay on the highway and hold sixty, at our pace, we can get on them in about 20twentyplus minutes."

"Soon, there's gonna be a shit-ton of units behind them," Lindner added. "Every municipality—Doral, Hialeah,

Hialeah Gardens, Miami Lakes—Highway Patrol is joining for sure. And if they hit Broward, it's gonna be crazy."

"Yeah, but we're PRT; they all know we're coming. If we can get there before the chase ends, we'll take point," Mateo responded.

From the engine's racing and occasional sudden braking, they could smell the heated rubber from the car's tires and the heated metal from the engine's temperature rising. The training never included this type of chase over such a long distance, but Mateo held to the fundamentals.

Hanging from the rearview mirror were Mateo's US Army Reserve dog tags. They swung from side to side, matching the car's movements—a subtle reminder that police work combined urban warfare where the enemy was usually an armed, sociopathic criminal.

Mateo was intently focused on catching up: he was burning through a lot of fuel, but he knew that the UPS truck was, too. He did the quick math in his head. If the truck was full and started on an early-morning route, it must have been close to half-empty, but so was his patrol unit. But Mateo's burn rate must have been three-to-one compared to the UPS truck. The longer the chase went, the greater the chance they would run dry before this chase ended. No time to think more about that, though.

Pedal to the metal.

By now, a Miami media outlet had its helicopter in the air, monitoring the publicly available police headquarters' radio frequency. Media pilots and reporters all know police codes and jargon. The pilot had a view from about 500 feet above. No air traffic to weave, dodge, or bob around; no stop signs, yield signs, or red lights either. These media helicopters were equipped with high-resolution cameras with zoom-in-and-out capability.

As soon as the media outlet was overhead the chase, it fed a livestream to its station, and it was "breaking news" for anyone to watch. Ironically, the media had a broader view of the unfolding events than the marked police units on the ground, now getting closer from behind.

Until the first police unit got the UPS truck in sight, the media chopper was relaying the information to the 911 dispatcher, and she, in turn, was retransmitting the location, direction, approximate speed, and lane changes.

5:20 p.m.

"Attention, all units, turn off your lights and sirens," said the dispatcher.

All pursuing officers knew why. This would allow unmarked units to stealthily approach the UPS truck from behind to confirm this was the right one; count how many subjects were in it and get their descriptions; and determine if they were still both armed, whether the hostage was still in the truck, and if they were alive. It would also answer an important question: Might one of the bad guys have taken his UPS uniform to make himself look like the hostage?

All of these questions required precise answers.

5:23 p.m.

A squad from MDPD's narcotics K-9 unit now picked up the chase, pushing their unmarked, dark-colored SUVs—fully blacked out—toward the UPS truck, now doing about seventy miles per hour. All marked units remained quiet and out of sight, at least a mile behind the truck.

The pursuit had carried them north on the Turnpike and then onto I-75. The truck was now only minutes from the Miami-Dade and Broward County line. Under the doctrine of fresh pursuit, jurisdiction wasn't an issue. It was a law that allowed continued jurisdiction outside of a police officer's otherwise lawful boundaries.

The UPS truck held the outermost lane. One unmarked SUV—driven by narcotics K-9 Sergeant Machado—eased up from several lanes to the left, keeping a low profile to avoid spooking the driver. Once parallel, the officer got a clear look inside: a Black male driving, armed; another Black male in the passenger seat, also armed; and a dark-skinned Hispanic male lying face down between them with a gun pressed to his head. The officer backed off to avoid detection.

Without warning, the UPS truck's passenger lunged out of the door and aimed his weapon directly at Machado's unmarked unit. Keeping the vehicle steady, she drew with her left hand, lowered her window, and fired two rounds at Hall. Both shots missed her.

"*Shots fired!*" her voice cut through the radio. It was immediately repeated by the dispatcher.

Every cop who heard it knew what that meant. It didn't matter who pulled the trigger or how many rounds were discharged—this was a game changer. Who fired and how many rounds didn't matter. If the shots came from the suspects, the ending was already written—*suicide by cop*. That was how it went when men cornered by consequence decided the law wouldn't take them alive.

In 1970, singer and songwriter R. Dean Taylor released a song that captured the mindset of a man barricaded and surrounded by police, one who had already served prison time and was determined not to return. Law enforcement officers, many of them likely too young to recognize "Indiana

Wants Me," nonetheless understood the suicidal-fatality mentality. The robbers in front of them were not amateurs. They were likely repeat offenders, men who had been convicted before and were prepared to do whatever was necessary to avoid going back.

If the gunfire came from law enforcement, it still meant an officer out there saw a threat too real, too immediate, to hesitate, and fired first. Either way, every responding officer knew that it meant that deadly force was now necessary and justified.

Every officer behind the wheel who heard the transmission understood those two words—*shots fired*. These subjects needed to stop, surrender, and let it be over. If they didn't, today was poised to end in a major gun battle.

"Jesus Christ, they are firing again!" Mateo said.

"Well, either that or law enforcement is! It's gonna get real bad," Lindner joined.

The unmarked units peeled off, making way for dozens of marked patrol cars that moved in behind and around the fleeing truck. The subjects now knew law enforcement was on them. More than a dozen marked units accelerated to join the pursuit, with many others close behind. The nearest PRT officer was Young.

They were now about five to ten minutes away. Lindner rechecked his rifle; one was confirmed in the chamber. He dropped the magazine just to make sure he was topped off and ensured that his red dot was aligned and secured on the frame. He tightened the straps on his tactical vest as he ran through his protocol checklist.

Mateo checked his own gear in sharp, alternating motions—one hand on the wheel, the other snapping down buckles and cinching straps. In doing so, he switched hands every second or two, compensating for their speed, keeping the car steady.

The plan was to encircle the moving truck, "contain" it, and force a gradual slowdown. The chase policy did not allow for PIT maneuver or a total block-off. The chased vehicle needed to have an exit route. But a rolling slowdown was permissible.

Officer Young closed in on the driver's side. The driver noticed him and fired several rounds at his unit. Officer Young took evasive action and announced another "Shots fired!" over the radio.

The challenge was the apparent purposeful speed of the UPS truck, higher than the posted speed limit. Traffic, while moderate, allowed the UPS truck to continuously approach slower-moving vehicles ahead to disrupt the formation and positions of the police vehicles. It appeared as if Louis saw that and regulated the speed to do exactly that, rendering this tactic useless. He was now a confirmed skilled tactician—criminal himself.

His cell phone rang—it was his girl, Leticia. She'd been watching the breaking news and had quickly put two and two together. "Honey...is that you in the UPS truck?" she asked, her voice trembling.

As it turned out, Leticia had called the police herself, indicating that she knew it was her husband in that truck.

"Turn yourself in," she pleaded.

"I'm in too deep," he responded.

The robbers now knew the chase was live on television, and there was no chance of escape. This put Ortiz's life in grave danger—they had nothing to lose by killing him or using him as a human shield. Dozens of police units were now closing in from all sides.

An MDPD helicopter hovered overhead, tracking every move and change in direction in orchestra-like fashion. A long prison term awaited them—life, maybe even *the death penalty* if Lilian and the hostage didn't both survive.

The driver then made a calculated move. He suddenly exited I-75 onto Pines Boulevard and headed east at a steady clip. He knew it was approaching rush hour and that the congestion would complicate any decisive police action. In heavy urban traffic, aggression became riskier for officers and civilians, giving them a better chance to stay alive and keep moving.

Units from multiple Broward County police agencies began converging and joining the chase. But that created an immediate serious tactical problem: communications. MDPD was on its own channel; each Broward agency was on theirs. Layer onto that the fact that every department had its own pursuit and use of force policing policy, compounding the chaos.

"He's heading into Century Village!" one officer shouted over the radio—a populated senior citizen community. A shooting in this elderly community would draw extreme criticism, no matter how it ended.

Louis blew through the main security gate without even tapping the brakes. He sliced straight through the development, crossed through several streets, and then went out the opposite side.

"Attention, all units, media is overhead," the dispatcher warned, reminding all officers that their every move was *now* on camera. To make sure they *all* got it, the dispatcher would repeat that announcement a bit later. It was a disguised way of saying, *Whatever you do, it will be recorded on video...wink, wink, nod, nod.*

The UPS truck weaved through traffic, navigating itself between stopped, moving, and turning cars. At times, to avoid stopping at or near an intersection, it veered off the roadways onto sidewalks and swales, or by making sudden U-turns even before approaching a congested intersection to avoid getting stuck and forcing it to come to a full stop.

With each passing second, it became increasingly clear there would be no surrender and this would be a firefight. The fluidity of the situation and non-unified police agency communications made any *plan* simply impossible.

Severely complicating matters was that the deadly threat was doubled—one on each side of the UPS truck. This heightened the risk of a crossfire scenario. They would have to "cup" their approach rather than use the traditional L. Also, with so many agencies involved, there was no single controlling command. Each officer did what they could—orderly following the truck, adapting to its erratic moves, and letting the suspects dictate what would happen next—an undesirable but inevitable release of control.

This called for a rare combination of patience, anticipation, and sharp alertness to an unfolding event that none of the dozens of officers had ever experienced, and for which no training exercise existed—not in the academy and not in any in-service course, not even within the PRT specialty training. So, the fundamentals mattered most. When this type of chaos took over, you had to go back to the basic training checklist for use-of-force, street survival, pursuit policies, and techniques.

IV
THE ACADEMY

Miami, 1980s

In 1979, Miami-Dade County launched a tourism campaign that quickly drew both acclaim and controversy. The slogan: *Miami. See It Like a Native.* Bold and quite risqué for its time.

Rick was now nineteen years old, and Paul had all he needed to bounce Rick from the Hialeah "BK Throne."

The centerpiece featured a model posed as a snorkeler. She wore a black bikini—just a bottom, no top—her long dark hair falling down her back, skin deeply tanned and lightly oiled. A pair of black flippers hung from her left hand. Her back faced the camera lens, head slightly tilted down, gaze fixed left to the ground below, the mask and snorkel sitting nicely on the top of her head. The image captured both allure and adventure, a daring invitation to experience Miami in a way few tourists had imagined or enjoyed before.

It was a nationwide tourist attraction campaign. In South Florida, it was everywhere—in magazines and newspapers, on buses and bus benches, at bus stations, and on billboards. You couldn't drive a mile without seeing that ad. Today, a signed poster from that limited run will set you back about $1,250 online.

Around the same time, the county launched another campaign, this one to recruit police officers. They picked a sharp-looking guy named Rob Haley—a recently graduated MDPD officer—as the face of it. The slogan read, *Wear the Silver Badge.* It was a huge hiring campaign.

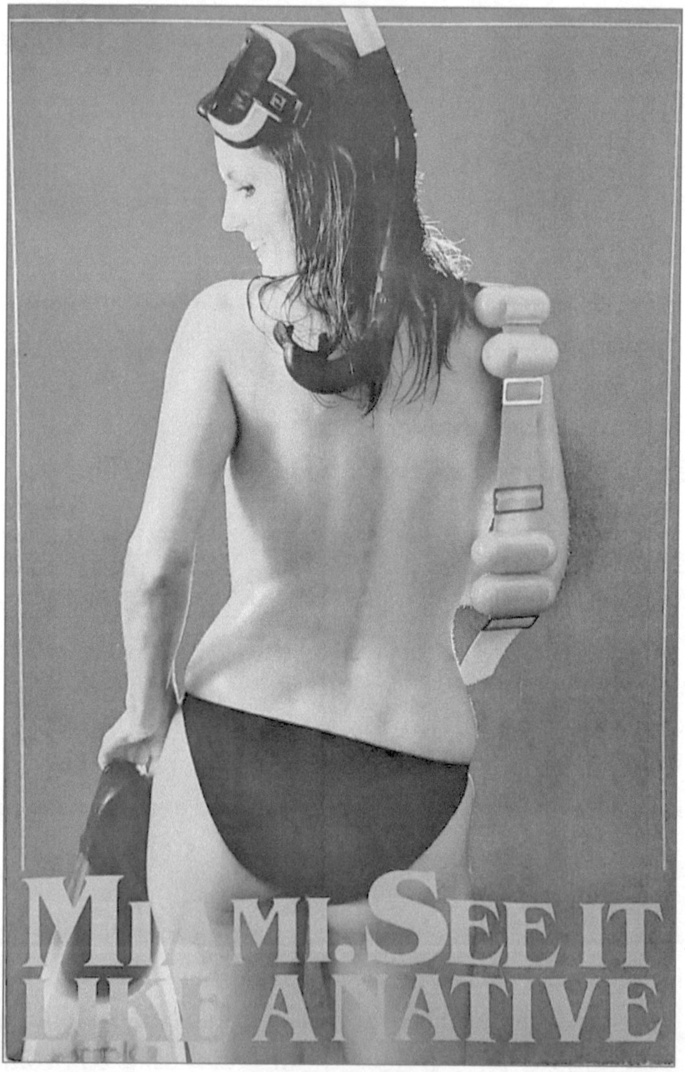

Nineteen eighty transformed Miami from a hit of a simple, sleepy, Southern town just waking up to emerge into the mega metropolis and international city it is today. Tourism was booming, as was the drug trafficking trade. People were putting down marijuana joints and the occasional 714 quaalude and picking up spoons and straws to snort cocaine. LSD and heroin were a thing of the past.

The white powder consumption was not just socially acceptable; it was sexy and fashionable. One hundred dollars a gram, $50,000 a kilo. Miami's skyline transformed mainly with drug trafficking cash, as it was not until 1987 that the federal money laundering statute passed. Cash—green cash—was everywhere and anywhere. Every jewelry store—yes, even Mayors—car dealer, and yacht dealer had cash-counting machines. And then there was a real Tony Montana in town—Jose Yero—a Cuban national bicycle champion. There were also, of course, *Willy and Sal*. Little did Rick know at the time, but he would cross paths with them in two very different ways over the next twenty years.

In April 1980, Miami was jolted awake—almost suddenly—by the Mariel boatlift—more than 100,000 Cuban migrants flooded into Key West, many of them hardened criminals. They were the Tren de Aragua of their era. Miami itself was the Caribbean's version of today's Dubai—flashy, fast, and flooded with money. Tourism boomed, and so did the violence, punctuated by the infamous Cocaine Cowboys shoot-out at Miami's Dadeland Mall in late 1979, in which the perpetrators employed machine guns while law enforcement officers still carried six-shot revolvers.

Rick's hiring by the Public Safety Department (PSD) was a no-brainer. He was barely nineteen, had no criminal record but a clean enough driving history, and was a disciplined martial artist. He breezed through both the polygraph and psychological evaluations. He didn't smoke, didn't drink—not even coffee—and kept himself in top physical shape. He was multilingual, focused, and squared away. He came with strong recommendations from active officers he'd done ride-alongs with, including Chief Keith Joy. Rick wasn't marginally qualified; he was a perfect fit and was built for the silver badge.

The police academy was located at the Miami-Dade Community College North Campus.

Day one was memorable. Rick's BLE class began with exactly seventy recruits; one-third made it to graduation.

Two of Rick's training advisors were former military—one from the United States Air Force, the other a former Army Special Forces Ranger—Sam Aguirre—stood out among them: tough as nails, a relentless son of a gun.

A few years later, Hollywood released a film called *An Officer and a Gentleman.* Its opening scene immediately reminded Rick of his day one—no recruit escaped the intimidation tactics. Like the film's protagonist, Zack Mayo, Rick was determined that he would not be weeded out. If Ruben Font couldn't break him, the academy training had less of a chance. He played the game well, confident and perhaps a little cocky.

At the academy, Rick noticed that every Basic Law Enforcement (BLE) class carried both a number and a self-selected title. His was BLE 49—"The Survivors."

Rick was certain he'd graduate—but he still chanced nothing. No one, except his family and a few close friends—including Keith—could know he'd made it to the police academy. Not yet. He still held the title of regional manager at BK, and if Ms. Sharpe found out, her plans for Paul would mature prematurely. How would he juggle both worlds?

Rick engineered a plan. He told the BK owner he was taking full-time classes at Miami-Dade Community College—

which, technically, was absolutely true—the college *was* giving Rick criminal justice program college credits for attending the academy.

Eventually, Rick told Sharpe that Paul was now ready to take over. Rick would step back, returning to night manager at the single store he had started at. A minor pay cut, but worth it. The owner seemed relieved that Rick beat her to a decision she was seemingly wrangling with for weeks.

Every afternoon, Rick left the academy at 4:50 p.m. and sped the short distance to BK. Before he pulled into the parking lot, he'd stop on a side street and change in the cramped privacy of his car—like Clark Kent—but it was the only way to keep his two professional worlds from colliding.

The secret nearly blew up in Rick's face one night when Keith, craving his Double Whopper with Cheese, walked into the BK and spotted Rick behind the counter.

Before Rick could intercept him, Keith blurted out, "Didn't you already start the academy?"

Rick's reflexes went into immediate defense mode; his mind snapped into gear instantly. The entire crew froze, eyes shifting toward him, curious, startled, confused.

He didn't flinch. "Nah, long story. I'll meet you in the dining room in a few and explain." His denial was, again, technically not a lie. He had not *started* the academy; he was now well into the six-month BLE program. Rick suspected that some of his coworkers knew, but no one ever explored their curiosity with a question.

Crisis contained. Disaster averted.

While at the academy, Rick's proficiency drew the attention of all of his training advisors. Three offers came: City of

Miami Police, Hialeah Police, and, surprisingly, the United States Secret Service. The police departments offered more money than the feds, but Rick wanted PSD—countywide jurisdiction, a massive department, real scope. The Secret Service tempted him with visions of protecting the president, but he didn't want to spend his first many years chasing money counterfeiters.

Six months after day one, Rick graduated—and was sworn in on the very same day. Only a third of his academy class graduated. The *Miami Herald* covered the ceremony. The *Wear the Silver Badge* promotion was still going strong. Front-page local news showed Rick's mother pinning on his badge beneath the headline: *A Mother's Pride*.

After arriving home, Rick typed up his resignation from BK. "As a result of my recent graduation at Miami-Dade Community College..." It was *technically* true. Besides his Florida Department of Law Enforcement certificate, Rick had also graduated with an associate's degree from the college in criminal justice.

Rick's first assignment was the *distinguished* Northeast District—"Station 6"—covering Aventura, Miami Beach, North Miami, and Norland. He was ordered to report on Tuesday at 0800 hours, Sundays and Mondays off.

When he pulled into the station's rear parking lot in his 1980 air-induction Camaro Z-28, two things struck him immediately. First, most of the officers drove pickup trucks—a stark contrast to his sporty muscle car—and there was no place to park it where it might go unnoticed.

Second, a green-and-white patrol unit rolled in, driven by a bald guy who looked like he came straight out of the set in *Kojak*—a police TV series starring Homicide Lieutenant Telly Savalas, whose character's delight was to suck on lollipops. Coffee in hand, he headed toward the rear entrance without a glance, radiating the quiet authority of someone who had seen everything *twice*.

Where am I? Rick thought to himself.

As Rick approached the station's rear door, he couldn't miss the sign posted above the threshold: *There is never a reason to be discourteous.*

He picked up his pace, trying to beat Kojak to the entrance—probably too obvious about it. But when Kojak reached for the keypad, Rick realized this wasn't just another officer. The gold badge and one gold rectangular bar on each of his uniform shirt collars gleamed—lieutenant—his name plate read *J. Waters*.

Everything about him was spit-shining and tight. Rick hit the call buzzer anyway. The lieutenant ignored that and tapped in the key code numbers—0006—with exaggerated calm, calling out each number as if reciting something only he was meant to know, and the door clicked open.

"Good morning, Lieutenant," Rick said.

Lieutenant Waters looked him up and down. "Let me guess, you must be the new Cuban rookie. Very sharp." He had a discerning, deep tone—a slow Southern drawl making him sound every bit the country boy.

Now up close, Rick could see what was really inside the white Styrofoam cup; it wasn't Waters's morning joe. Instead, he used it to discard the tobacco he was chewing.

"Your name tag spells D-I-A-Z. How do you pronounce that? *Die-ass*?"

"No, sir, you were close; the *i* is like two *e*'s. And the *z* is like the *z* in 'Zulu.' It's *Dee*-az."

"The first initial on your nameplate says R. What's your first name? Ricardo?"

"No, sir, it's Richard," Rick replied.

Waters squinted at him, then cracked a short laugh.

"Richard? That's not a Cuban name. You sure it's not 'Ricardo'?" He let the joke hang for a beat. A moment of silence followed. "I'm kidding," Waters finally said. "Welcome to the district."

This guy was a real redneck, but he still wore the gold bars—a rank that demanded a ton of respect.

Rick held his tongue. "Sir, I was born in Miami, and my dad is Cuban, but my mom's blonde with blue eyes—a traditional American, or *gringa,* as us Cubans would say."

"Well, that explains the *Richard,*" the lieutenant said. "Anyway, I hear you did real good in the academy, but the true test is what you do on the street. And that you speak Spanish fluently. We can certainly use that here at Station 6—more Latinos are moving into the district every year. Lesson number one—here, you'll be called by your last name. Diaz. Did I get it right this time?"

"Yes, sir," Diaz answered.

"Lesson two," Waters said with a half-smirk, nodding toward the entrance. "Cut the door-butler act. Nobody here's impressed by brown-nosers. Just do your job and you'll fit in."

He paused, then added, "It'll take a while, so be patient. We get about one rookie a month. The last few this year have been disappointing—one was terminated for insubordination. Frankly, we saved him from himself. It left a squad already shorthanded, but keeping him would've been a bigger mistake. Beats me how he made it through the academy."

"Yes, sir," said Diaz.

"You're very early, but roll call is down the hall to your right. You're excused!"

"Thanks, Lieutenant," Rick said as he skipped away.

He thought he heard the lieutenant mutter, "Fucking rookies." Strangely, Rick wasn't offended; he understood—especially as he stopped to look at the patrol division board near the front desk.

A close look at the "Platoon Personnel Board" on the wall showed 152 uniformed patrol officers—and only three apparent Hispanic last names: Fernandez, Hernandez, and Lora. Diaz would later learn that only one of them spoke enough Spanish to hold even a one-minute conversation.

The station had an orderly yet clear "cowboy air" about itself. Shotguns stood neatly in rows, handheld radios sat upright on their thin chargers, everything was perfectly in its place.

By week's end, it was apparent to Rick that of the 152, there were maybe fifteen Black officers; fewer women; no Asians; no Haitians; no Jamaicans; a few Italian last names. Most patrol officers were white males, six feet tall, and more than half of them looked like weight lifters. *Big* bastards.

Rick got it really clear now. This was a shitkicker, good-ol'-boy district. The pickup trucks were the first signal, but the exchange with the lieutenant and now this personnel chart nailed the district's personality.

Rick learned early that morning that they'd only call you by your first name if they really liked and trusted you—or if you'd been around long enough to earn it by long-term seniority.

He entered the roll call room and met his new sergeant, John Browne—mustached, tall, thin, with a warm smile that carried a quiet authority. The greeting was pleasant and professional. There were six officers on the squad, most of them field training officers wearing a small silver FTO plate on their shirts just below their name tags. Diaz would earn one himself not long after that memorable day.

Four of the squad members held Styrofoam cups, but only one actually had coffee. The other three were packing their lips with chew, grinding it around, and spitting into the cups with dull, wet plunks. The stench rising off them was a mix of burnt coffee and fermented spit. It caught Diaz off guard; he'd never seen anything like it before. It didn't feel like Miami-Dade County—it felt more like Lubbock, Texas or Tucson, Arizona.

Sergeant Browne assigned Rick to FTO Robert Lester. Roll call went as Rick expected, and by 8:20 a.m., they were filing out to the rear lot to load up their patrol cars. Lester said he'd drive. It all seemed so routine to him, but not to Rick. It was just the opposite.

"Diaz, how are you with the radio?" Lester asked.

"Pretty good," Diaz answered, understating the burden of his response.

They followed the routine checklist, climbed into the white-and-green unit, and rolled out of the station.

"Check us in on the radio. Our unit number is 6123."

Diaz waited for a break in radio traffic, keyed the mic, and, with no hesitation, spoke clearly: "Six-one-two-three."

A moment later came the dispatcher's reply: "Six-one-two-three, QSK"—*Go ahead.*

"Show me two officers, 09 [in service], from 156th and the Boulevard," Diaz said. He was letting Dispatch know they were a two-man unit and officially in service, ready to take calls and departing the station.

They merged northbound onto Biscayne Boulevard, cruising at patrol speed—always below the limit.

"Not bad," Lester quipped.

Only a few moments later, Lester and his rookie were approaching a bus stop, maybe fifty yards ahead. A woman standing about fifty feet away suddenly picked up the pace, and for no apparent reason—at least to Rick's eyes—walked briskly toward it, but there wasn't any bus in sight. To Diaz, it seemed a bit odd, but nevertheless insignificant; to Lester, it was enough to raise suspicion.

She looked to be around twenty-five, wearing tight cut-off blue jeans. A semi-see-through blouse tied at the bottom exposed a few inches of her midriff. Her heels were high enough for a gala event, and they looked brand-new. She wasn't particularly attractive, but not bad to look at either. She was not classy-looking but did not fit the cheap-looking profile of a prostitute.

Lester slowed down and pulled off the roadway, bringing the patrol car to a stop. He briskly stepped out—six-foot-two, blond, blue eyes, with a bushy mustache. Like most MDPD officers on Rick's squad, he was built like a bodybuilder. Rick would later learn that he was a professional powerlifter.

"Good morning. How are you? Mind if I ask if you have any weapons on you?" Lester said.

"I'm good. I ain't got no weapons on me. And if you really wanna pat me down, I'd rather a lady cop do it. Why you messin' with me anyway?"

Lester knew the preference was just that—a preference, not a rule. Her clothes were wrapped so tightly around her body, it was obvious she wasn't carrying a gun. Still, he went ahead with a quick and very superficial outer-garment frisk, the kind the Supreme Court signed off on in *Terry v. Ohio*.

Cops liked the "good" high-count cases—the ones that let them do their jobs; *Terry* was one of them. On the other hand, they disliked *Miranda*.

"Are you waiting for the bus?" Lester asked.

She said she was.

"While we're waiting for it, can I see some ID?"

She had none.

"What's your name and date of birth?"

Silence.

She finally gave him a name and date of birth, and Lester quickly jotted them down on the palm of his hand.

Rick, meanwhile, wasn't quick enough to pull out his pocket-size department notepad for his own use.

"Ever been arrested?"

Silence again.

After a few minutes, she responded. "Yes—for misdemeanor bullshit stuff. Never convicted, though. I ain't got zero convictions."

"That's a double negative," said Lester.

"You know what I mean," she added. "I got some arrests, but no convictions."

Lester just slowly shook his head side to side, fighting his own impatience. She was smart; he had to be careful.

Lester ordered Rick to run a background check on her through the police computer via radio. "This won't take long," he told her.

"Well, if the bus gets here, I'm getting on. I'm not under arrest," she said.

"Ma'am, if you have no warrants, you're good to go. Like I said, this should be quick—and there's no bus in sight."

The report came back fast: multiple arrests for prostitution and loitering and prowling, one for resisting arrest without violence—but as she'd said, no convictions.

"What's your address?" Lester asked.

"Officer, you know I don't have to answer that. I've been arrested before—I know my rights. I can explain why I'm here, and that's all I have to do. This is a public bus bench. You can't arrest me. I'm waiting for the bus." She rolled her eyes. "Man, ain't you got better stuff to do? Go get a coffee or a donut."

Lester chuckled. "You hear that attitude, Diaz?"

Lester then turned to the woman, "Look, ma'am, I hear

you. We've had several complaints about prostitution in this area—and car break-ins, too. My rookie here's in training, so I'm just having him fill out a field interrogation form for intelligence purposes."

"Well, you got what you asked for. And I ain't your rookie's training puppet. Oh, shit! Guess what? Here comes the bus! How convenient! Aren't you gonna ask me where I'm going?"

"Sure, but I wouldn't expect you'd answer," Lester answered.

"So where *are* you headed?" Lester asked.

She flashed a quick grin. "None of your fucking business—that's your answer. I know my rights. You can't force me to answer that. And the law don't require me to be nice to you—only to obey a lawful order, and I ain't hearing one. Goodbye!"

Rick and Lester, temporarily speechless, exchanged a look—half frustration, half disbelief.

"Wise-ass," Lester said under his breath. "You'll meet all kinds out here," he muttered, eyes following her as she climbed onto the bus.

Rick said nothing, but the rookie's expression said enough: *Was that normal?*

Lester didn't say anything; he just shook his head and pulled back onto the road. "Well, we got our first stat of the day!"

"What?" Rick asked.

Lester laughed. "One ticket, one FI card, and one arrest a day keeps the sergeant away."

Ah. Rick let out a low hum and nodded. He understood. Lester was talking about *quotas*.

"I thought officers weren't supposed to have quotas," Rick said.

"Yeah—well, a cop will never admit that. But if one month, you make twenty arrests—one a day—and your evaluation comes back *satisfactory*, then the next month you make ten and suddenly it's *unsatisfactory*, what does that tell you?"

No response.

"Hey, what are the three basic rules?" Lester asked.

Rick responded without a beat, "Make sure you go home every day; don't get wet; and don't go hungry."

"Well done!" Lester said. "Who taught you that?"

"Long story," Rick said.

An hour later, the radio crackled to life. "Six-one-two-three," the dispatcher called.

Lester let Rick reach for the mic. "Six-one-two-three, go ahead."

"Oh-five," she replied. An 05 meant return to the station.

"Shit," Lester muttered.

Rick figured that maybe Lester had forgotten something, needed to sign a report—something administrative. They pulled into the station, walked through the front lobby, and were buzzed in.

The desk sergeant—a Southern boy probably counting down the days to retirement, reading the newspaper without lifting his eyes, said, "The major wants to see you upstairs."

Lester took a step toward the nearby elevator.

"Not you, the rookie," the sergeant added. "Red seems pissed about something. He didn't say it, but you took a 10 at 166th and Biscayne, right? It's probably about that. What the fuck happened?"

A 10 was code for a stop, area search, or citizen encounter.

"That bitch made a complaint?" Lester said.

"Yep," the sergeant replied. "Just have a little talk with the rookie before he sees the major."

Lester took Rick outside, away from the front desk and the curious stares. He lit a cigarette, took a slow drag, and said, "Listen, kid—relax. We didn't do anything wrong. She looked suspicious, and she looked like she was avoiding us. That's enough for an investigative stop any day." He tapped ash off the end of his cigarette, eyes narrowing a little. "The problem isn't the BS complaint. It's the politics."

The major was a political player—real smooth talker. He was very connected with the rich Jews in Aventura and Turnberry. Big-money folks in all of North Miami Beach loved him. He usually came to roll call on a rookie's first day. Anyway, his name was Erwin Heller, but everyone called him "Red."

He flicked the ash again, studying Rick. "Be careful in there. Whatever he asks, just answer the question. The more you explain, the more you are losing. Don't kiss his ass. That doesn't fly around here."

The pattern of the district profile was becoming clearer by the hour.

Rick straightened his posture, his tone calm but firm. "I'm not afraid. I know what happened, and I'm not a hand-up. I got this."

Lester smirked. "We'll see, rookie." He seemed more bothered than concerned.

Rick hoped he was right.

He rode the elevator to the second floor. As the doors slid open, a woman in her late thirties waiting there greeted him with a polite nod. Rick could feel his blood pressure rising.

The room beyond was alive in function but dead in spirit—detectives in plain clothes hunched over their desks, bristling through reports or talking on the phone. It was busy but contractual. Rick compared the environment around him to the ones he had watched for years on police television shows. He had grown up on *Adam-12* and *Starsky & Hutch*.

A handful of secretaries were typing feverishly but quietly nearby. Most of the detectives were on the phone, a couple with their feet upon their desks—they must have had a lot of seniority. It was a large, windowless space—rows of desks lined up face-to-face, the walls, baseboards, and floor all a boring beige, the furniture a dull brown. Anything but warm and welcome. The only pulse in that room came from the people working inside it. But all of their heads rose, the rookie on day one being hauled into Red's office only one hour into the shift.

"Rick?" Strangely, she didn't say "Officer Diaz."

That was odd, Rick thought to himself. "Yes, ma'am."

It was the first time anyone had called him "Rick" that day—but it was still early.

"I'm Lou Ann, Major Heller's secretary." She looked him over with a faint hint of attraction that caught Rick off guard. He was about ten years younger than her. *Could she be...?* he wondered.

Lou Ann wore no wedding ring. Must have been divorced. Rick was single, and Lou Ann probably knew it from reviewing his file. She was every bit as country as Kojak and the rest of them, only she didn't chew tobacco. Regardless, Rick was not inclined toward the "Western world."

Rick would later learn what she was really interested in was his eligibility for her almost eighteen-year-old daughter. She tried to set them up—*twice*. Just what Rick needed: a rookie on probation, dating a minor whose mother worked for the major.

She tested Rick with a smirk and snarky remark. "Y'all look the same crispy way the first few days. Then the shoes get scuffed, the uniform wrinkles, and the shine starts to dull. A few years later, the belly starts to show."

"Not me," Rick replied.

"Yeah, yeah. Follow me."

Rick and Lou Ann walked down the hallway to the very end, passing her desk—the nameplate *Major Secretary* sat equidistant in the center, and its surface could be no tidier. Military precision.

Lou Ann knocked twice on the closed office door bearing a brass placard that read: *Major "Red" Erwin Heller*. So, he really did embrace the nickname.

"Bring 'em in, Lou Ann," a voice called from inside.

As soon as Rick walked into the office, Major Heller stood up. He set down the pipe he'd been puffing, a faint trace of cherry tobacco still curling in the air.

Rick recognized the scent instantly—*finally*, an officer who didn't smoke nasty, cheap cigarettes or chew tobacco.

As Rick fully stepped inside, it was night and day. The space was big, somewhat intimidating, tailored to the elderly man who occupied it—refined, yet commanding. One wall was lined with awards and framed commendations from every unit he had ever served in, each piece polished and perfectly aligned. A thick crystal cigar tray rested on a side table, surrounded by an assortment of ornate lighters, each one looking like it might have a story.

The major didn't pull a power move and wait for Rick to approach. He stood up, walked toward Rick, and met him halfway across the room. Was it calculated? It certainly felt that way. His orange hair and freckled face explained the nickname well enough—probably given to him as a kid and carried proudly for fifty-five years or so.

"Welcome to Station 6. We've been eager to meet you."

"Glad to make your presence, Major," Rick said, his tone

respectful. He purposefully did not say more than "Glad to be here, sir."

"I would've met you at roll call, but I had an early meeting—with a bagel, a coffee, and a friend. Rascal House. If you don't know it, you will. It's a bit out of the district, but worth the drive. It's the one place you can go outside in the district without needing supervisory approval. Just don't announce that you are there on the radio if you don't have to."

"Never been there, sir, but if you recommend it, I will check it out."

"Kid, we don't need kiss-asses here. If you really hate bagels, or Jewish deli food, just say so."

"No, sir, I love a good bagel. I just don't drink coffee."

The message was clear. Brown-nosing wasn't just unwelcome here—it was despised.

By the second day, Rick was learning fast. He absorbed all procedures like a sponge. His radio skills were impeccable, mirroring those of a seasoned officer. He had the fundamentals down pat, but what truly impressed Sergeant Browne—and the rest of the squad—was how quickly he learned and adapted, but most of all, how well he wrote. His reports were sharp, detailed, and written with precision beyond their own skills.

Rick's education explained it. He'd studied at King's College—a British school in Madrid, Spain—and by age fifteen had completed all requirements to graduate. His writing wasn't just good—it was refined and exquisite. The language carried weight, the rhythm confident, the style polished enough to rival any seasoned author. He received full academic scholarships to both Oxford and Cambridge—arguably the two most prestigious universities in England. He passed them up and instead returned to the United States in mid-1975 when his parents—through a historical and political event—were abruptly dismissed from their posts abroad.

With the death of Spain's dictator, General Francisco Franco, King Juan Carlos I had ordered all foreign workers terminated to open jobs for Spanish nationals and curb unemployment.

When Rick returned home, he was told he'd need to start the tenth grade. He didn't argue—he simply handed over his transcripts and test scores. After taking an IQ test and presenting proof of his academic record and scholarships, Miami Senior High handed him a high school diploma.

On day three, Lester's routine, habit, and practice had become boring. It was similar to days one and two—the same boring and unpleasant stop, walk, and search the men's public bathroom at Greynolds Park. An occasional traffic stop, a truancy arrest, an FI card, a false alarm call, and a traffic accident. No action.

In the police world—much like in the military—officers often earned nicknames or call signs. Before they left roll call that morning, one of the officers on the squad whispered to Rick that Lester's was "The Dirt Monster." At first, Rick didn't know why, but he would not long later.

Every morning around nine, Lester would park outside Greynolds Park, step out of his cruiser, and slip into the dusty, dirty wooded trails leading to the men's restrooms. It was a known hangout for homosexual encounters, and Lester took pride in catching men in the act. The arrests rarely held up in court—two consenting adults, no money exchange, and privacy behind a closed stall didn't make for much of a case. Still, he'd charge them with sex in a public park and call it a win.

Call signs and nicknames came from the officer's reputation, habits, quirks, or stories that stuck. Some took years to earn one. It simply had to be "fitting." Lester was quite appropriately called "The Dirt Monster."

One day, Rick might get his.

V
THE SURVIVOR

Friday was day four. It was about 8:30 a.m., and a uniformed off-duty officer, Greg Lopez, was working at the People's Trust Bank and called in for a brief break—a 10—to get a cup of coffee across the street. The call was dispatched to Unit 6123, Rick and Lester's unit. They were en route when the silent alarm to the bank was triggered.

Lester muttered under his breath, "No way. Bank's just opening, and Lopez, the off-duty officer, is there. Somebody probably accidentally tripped the alarm." He shook his head. "The alarm company will clarify or Lopez will advise."

Still, he sped up a bit, continuing toward the bank, which was five minutes away at normal speed. Business and residential alarms were routine; ninety-nine times out of a hundred, they were false. But as they got around the bank's corner, with no notification from the alarm company or the officer, Lester pressed the gas pedal down. Something *felt* wrong. Nobody had called off the alarm dispatch as accidental. No emergency lights or siren, no screeching tires, no pulling up to the front; the approach was designed for stealth.

"You take the front, I'll get the back," Lester said, voice clipped. He pushed the cruiser harder. They slipped off the road and tucked the unit out of sight of the bank's main entrance doors that faced east.

Lester killed the engine and drew his revolver.

Rick mirrored the motion and pulled his revolver from his right-side holster. This time, the sound of the safety snap struck differently—it carried weight. This wasn't a drill.

As he pushed the gun forward through the breakfront aperture, the familiar clapping sound now sounded different than at the firearms range in training, hollow and deep, in a way that made everything feel heavier. His grip tightened around the new rubberized Pachmayr grip handles he'd installed just five days earlier. He hadn't fired with them yet, and for a brief second, that thought cut through his focus, but then Rick forced it out.

Too late now to pop on the original wooden stock grips he'd grown accustomed to. This was now likely an in-progress armed robbery. If so, where was the off-duty officer? Could he be dead or alive? No "shots fired" had been announced, nor any heard—at least not *yet*.

In the academy, they drilled a rule: Assume hostages are dead or will likely die; go after the threat; confront it; use the level of force reasonably necessary to neutralize it. The cherished Blue Max shooting medal Rick earned for the highest marksmanship at the academy now meant nothing.

Rick kept his breathing steady as he scanned the entryway, eyes moving over every reflection and shadow. He didn't know what waited on the other side—only that he had to find out. From outside, everything looked normal.

The sun was at his back, throwing his reflection across the glass doors like a target. Anyone inside could see him before he ever saw them. He knew he was going in blind. There was no academy drill for this. No perfect angle, no safe approach. Maybe the vest would stop a round—maybe not, but not going in wasn't an option. *Alone*, but he needed to move low, fast, quietly, and unseen.

Rick had to go in blinded by the glare reflecting off the double front doors. He slowly pushed the door open, crossing the threshold, and saw he had no cover. No turning back now. Besides his training, he had a six-shot revolver, two spare six-round speed-loaders on his belt, a vest—and three mundane days with his FTO.

A second set of glass doors separated the vestibule from the lobby. Rick gently pushed them, but they resisted. He jammed his radio into its holder and used both hands to push them open, using the sole of his left shoe to slow the closing doors behind him—no noise, no alarm.

It shut softly.

The transition from the bright Florida sun at Rick's rear to the dim interior in front of him was far more blinding than he expected. His eyes fought to adjust as he fought the panic that wanted to set in.

In the academy training, they taught you to shield your eyes before entering a dark area—but that was for a totally darkened room; this wasn't that. Covering his eyes for even a second here could be suicide. The lobby was small, sterile, offering no real cover—just a high-top counter where customers filled out deposit slips.

Rick crouched low, lowering his profile—to make himself a smaller target—and swept his revolver ahead, quickly panning the room.

Only one person was visible: a woman behind the teller counter. Her body was frozen. Her eyes met Rick—and they grew wide. Her look was terrified; it told Rick everything he needed to know. This was a robbery, and Lopez was likely dead.

Rick pressed a finger to his lips, signaling her to stay quiet. He gestured subtly with his arms raised, asking for the robbers' location.

She quietly looked down and to her right.

Rick motioned for her to move away slowly.

She understood immediately and followed his lead.

Before Rick could move toward the teller's counter, a man in a ski mask popped up beside her and leveled his gun at him. At the same time, another masked robber burst from a hallway into the lobby, wielding two pistols—one in each hand—both aimed straight at him.

Rick had no cover. The robbers had the clear advantage—they had Rick surrounded and one was closing in. But Rick had always been a survivor, taking after his BLE class motto. Staying put to be executed wasn't how he'd go down, and surrendering could mean a likely death as well.

Rick landed on one desperate solution. He stayed low, darted right, then left, then right again—zigzagging across the lobby. Rounds tore past his head so close he felt the air snap against his ears. His end was near, and he wondered what it would feel like.

Rick had a millisecond for a single thought—the *Miami Herald* article less than a week old: *A Mother's Pride.* The image of his mother smiling in that photo would be his last living memory—he was sure of it.

Both robbers fired their weapons in Rick's direction, hitting everything around Rick from behind. The glass doors exploded, shards sparking into his face, causing disorientation and temporary blindness. Still, he kept moving on pure instinct.

There was only one chance, one direction that meant life—*out.* The sound inside the tiled lobby was deafening. Rick dove through the shattered door and made it to cover outside the bank.

Rick yanked his radio and pressed the key button. "It's 29 [robbery], shots fired!" he shouted.

Static.

By now, Lester had heard the gunfire—and Rick's radio transmissions confirmed it.

The dispatcher hit the emergency signal, "Attention, all units, 29 in progress, shots fired, 18320 West Dixie Highway, People's National Bank..."

Seconds after Rick found cover right outside the bank, both robbers burst through the front doors, one of them shielding himself behind the off-duty officer held hostage.

The air immediately exploded in gunfire—rapid, deafening chaos. Between twenty and thirty rounds were exchanged between officers and the robbers within only a few seconds. The two subjects and Officer Lopez were down.

Then—*silence.*

"Cease fire!" Rick yelled.

Rick first checked on Lopez. Miraculously, he was unharmed. One robber appeared dead. The other lay on the pavement, bleeding out, hit multiple times but still breathing.

Lester called out on his radio. "Fire Rescue on a 3, multiple-gunshot wounds, two subjects, officers QRU."

The smell of burnt gunpowder filled the air; blood was pooling around the subjects. Sirens grew louder as more backup units and rescue crews arrived. EMTs rushed in, working quickly on the surviving suspect—cutting open his shirt, packing wounds, and pushing fluids.

As the gun smoke thinned, adrenaline slowly dissipated and reality set in. The gunfight was over, but the aftermath was almost as chaotic. A full roll call went out, and every officer was accounted for. No injuries, no casualties.

Could there be more robbers—or victims—inside? Rick

and a backup officer moved back in, clearing the bank corner by corner.

No more threats. No civilian injuries. Just gun smoke odor, smoke settling, broken glass, shattered shell casings, and the aftermath of survival.

Rick led the teller outside, wrapped her in a blanket, and handed her an orange juice from his lunch box.

"How did you not get hit? They shot so many times."

Rick looked down, brushing away leftover shards of glass from his uniform, and said quietly, "I don't know either."

On-scene officers moved with urgency, some cordoning off the scene, securing evidence, others shouting over one another.

Then, cutting through the noise, a voice yelled, firm, commanding, and close, "Diaz! We need you to accompany Fire Rescue with one of the subjects to the hospital. Stay with the subject—he's alive; he's not dead."

Rick thought otherwise, as he was shot up pretty good.

Rick jumped into the back of the rescue truck—his first time in one. It looked like a mobile trauma bay. The subject was cuffed, strapped to a gurney, bleeding through bandages.

The rear door slammed shut, and almost as quickly, three hard knocks came from the outside door—the truck stopped.

"Now what?" muttered one of the paramedics.

The rear doors burst open. Officer Vince Farina appeared—"Kid, what the fuck are you doing?"

"I was told to escort the 39 [prisoner] to the hospital with Fire Rescue," Rick answered.

"Not like that, you're not." Farina climbed in, his unscuffed shoes thudding on the metal floor. They were brand-new or sure looked like it. "Draw your fucking gun. Cock it. Point it at that fucker. If he moves toward you, or tries to get away, shoot him. You hear me?"

"Yes, sir," said Rick.

Farina turned to the waiting paramedics seated up front. "You guys good with that?"

One of them nodded.

"He just robbed a bank and shot at you guys, right?" the driver asked.

"Fucking A, we're fine with that," the other medic added.

"Let's see it," snapped Farina.

Diaz unsnapped his Smith & Wesson revolver, cocked the hammer, cupped the grip with both hands, and aligned it to the left side of the suspect's head.

Farina clapped loudly near the robber's head. "Hey—you hear that?"

The suspect groaned, eyes half-open.

Farina whispered in his ear just enough for him to hear him but not the paramedics. "You better hope there's no bumps in the road."

Farina jumped out, slammed the door, then reopened it halfway. "Hey, kid..." He paused. "You did real good. We will meet up later."

With two quick pats on Diaz's knee, he said, "I am an FTO on afternoons; you are on day shift now, but going to afternoons next. You're doing your Phase 2 with me. And you guys—" he said, pointing at the paramedics. "No rush. He's not worth it."

The suspect was rolled into the ER, still cuffed.

A doctor glanced at him and said, "He's in bad shape. I don't think he'll make it, and he's fighting. I will give him some heavy meds."

Rick positioned himself beside the gurney, his gun now holstered but hand-ready. "Don't worry, doc. I've got orders. He's not moving—and neither am I. Just clear out if he tries something stupid."

Anger now simmered in Rick. He paused to remember the sign above the front door of the station. *There's never a reason to be discourteous.*

"Not now," he said to himself.

Hours later, Rick was relieved and ordered back to the station. He was directed straight to Red's office.

This time, Lou Ann wasn't waiting by the elevator. She spotted him the second the doors opened.

"Hey, Rick, you know where to go, right? He's anxious to talk to you. No rookie sees the major twice in one week."

Rick thought he'd followed his training—maybe he wasn't supposed to go in?

"I don't think you're in trouble," Lou Ann said, catching his expression.

Red came out of his office and called him in. "It's okay, Lou Ann, take that call on the line and hold all of mine."

He signaled to Rick, and they went inside the office. Nothing seemed to have moved in the past days. Red didn't sit; Rick stood face-to-face with the major.

"You've had quite a week, young man. Twice in this office. Sit down. Let's talk."

Rick felt a little relief after what Farina and Lou Ann had told him, yet the anticipation was overwhelming.

Red lit his pipe. He was focused, patient, drawing slowly as he put out the match he'd used to light the tobacco. Maybe the lighters were just decorative memories. The aroma of pipe smoke filled the office. He swished the smoke from his pipe. "I apologize—does the smoke bother you? I should have asked," he added, wafting it deliberately.

Rick noted the gesture, recognizing an opening—a small

bridge to connect. "Cigarette smoke bothers me, but I like Borkum Riff Cavendish Cherry. That's the pipe tobacco my father smokes."

"He's Cuban?"

"Yes, sir."

"He must smoke cigars, too, then."

"Actually, no, he doesn't."

"How about you, do you smoke?"

"No, sir."

"Good for you. Don't start. Ever try to? No?"

"No, sir. Not even one cigarette."

"Not even marijuana, ever?"

"Nope. They asked me that in the polygraph, and I said no—and I passed."

Red smiled faintly. "All right, then." He took another puff. We got off topic. Have you spoken to Scott Allen or Sergeant Browne yet?"

"No, sir. Who's Scott Allen?"

"He's our psychologist."

Rick froze. "A psychologist? Why?"

"It's due to the shooting, it's SOP [standard operating procedure]. You will be ROD [relieved of duty] three days and he will evaluate your mental fitness."

Rick was crestfallen. Was he being set up for termination? On probation, no real cause was needed. What would Dr. Allen be looking for? Fear? Bravado? Rick was twisted on what the right or wrong answers should be.

"Sir, now that you mention it, maybe I did see him... The name does sound a bit familiar—if he did my psych evaluation when I applied. I'll need to see him again?"

Red nodded. "Yes. You're not suspended. You're on admin. Getting off the road for a few days will be good for you—and for me. I'm going to have you work directly with me up here. I've seen some of your reports; your writing skills are impressive. You'll be reviewing some of mine due to the division chief. Maybe you can teach me how to write better?"

Rick exhaled slowly. "Got it, sir." This seemed to suggest that the Dr. Allen interview would be a mere formality for him.

"I'd love to ask you about the shooting," Red continued. "But by IA rules and *Garrity*, I cannot."

Garrity was a court case whose opinion now protects officers from being compelled to give a statement until after an investigation concludes.

"I can tell you that going into that bank alone today was ballsy. But let me ask you a hypothetical question off the record: If you were the FTO with a first-day rookie, would you have done everything the same?"

"No, sir," Rick said.

"We both agree; he should have gone in with you—together. So, the question is, do you feel comfortable with him as your FTO going forward?"

"Sir, I'm okay staying with him—it would be awkward. I've got three more weeks with him. Somebody needed to go in, and he's my FTO. I was not going to disobey his command."

"That's precisely why everyone around here is upset. Both of you should have entered the front, plain and simple. Anyways, you are excused. See Scott Allen, he's downstairs. You did everything right."

"Loud and clear, Major," Rick replied.

"By the way, Lou Ann wants to introduce you to her daughter. Cute as a button—but don't get any ideas. She's a minor. And Lou Ann is like a sister to me, so don't do anything stupid. See you tomorrow."

"Sir, yes, sir!" Rick saluted with a half-grin. They understood each other.

"Hey, Rick. Scott Allen."

"Hi, I remember you," Diaz said.

"Well, if you're here, you passed my evaluation. This won't take long. Off the record, it was a good shooting. What we discuss here is 100 percent doctor-patient privileged—not even the county will know. Understand?"

"Sure," Rick replied.

"After a traumatic event like an OIS—officer-involved shooting—officers can experience something called PTSD: post-traumatic stress disorder. So, let's get right to it. Tell me how you're feeling?" Allen asked.

"Good," Rick quickly responded.

"Anything more to add?"

"Nope."

"One guy died today; two, if the other one doesn't make it."

"Well, it's good that nobody in the bank was hurt and none of us were injured either, right?"

"How about the two subjects? They might have had families..." the psych asked.

Silence hung thick in the room. Rick's voice tightened. "Wait...you don't think the rest of us do, too? The bank employees...the officers? Who decided to do the armed robbery this morning? Me? No! Instead, I got up to come to work, not rob a damn bank. Have you ever been in a shoot-out, doctor?"

Allen didn't answer.

"I thought so... Look, let's cut through the bullshit. What's the deal here? I'm on probation—am I in trouble or getting fired?"

"If this happened again, would you do the same?"

"Absolutely." Rick did not hesitate.

"Okay. But I still can't clear you today. For the rest of the shift, you'll be working with Red upstairs. You're off Sunday and Monday. You'll be back Tuesday, full duty."

"But the major wanted me assigned to him for those days!" Rick exclaimed.

"He probably forgot your days off. You're cleared, kid. I'll sign you off." Dr. Allen leaned over, extending a white business card with his name embossed in sharp blue letters across the top. "If you want to talk more about it, here's my card."

"Sure," Rick said, fearing a further response could only make matters worse. He remembered Lester's warning, *The more you explain, the more you are losing.* When Rick got home, the card went right into the trash bin.

The next morning, the *Miami Herald* headline read: *Bank Robbery Ends in Bloodshed—Questions Raised Over Police Response.* Rick was furious; the prejudgment was perplexing.

The story painted the scene as if excessive force had been used, the tone suggesting the officers had gone too far. To Rick, it felt like the press had already picked a side, and it wasn't for the police. It was a rude awakening. He'd nearly died in that bank, and yet somehow, PSD's response was being criticized by some uninformed asshole Herald writer.

Later that day, a veteran officer from the district requested to meet with Unit 6123 a few blocks from the station. The officer motioned for Lester to stay in the car. He leaned into the open window. "Mind if I talk to your rookie for a minute?"

Lester shrugged, chewing on his toothpick, and waved

Rick out. Rick stepped out of the patrol car and approached him.

"I'm David," he said, lowering his voice. "I was off yesterday, but word travels fast. Everybody's talking about the 29 at People's Bank. And it's not good for Lester."

He shook his head and appeared disgusted. "You *never* leave your partner like that. He should've gone in with you—watch your back."

His posture eased. "Anyway...I wanted to meet you in person. Welcome to the district."

Rick was starting to absorb the impact of what real police work was and that not all officers were alike despite wearing the same uniform. It was nothing like *Kojak*, *Adam-12*, or *Starsky & Hutch.*

The next three weeks were uneasy. Strangely, Lester never spoke of the bank robbery—and neither did Rick. Around the station, the usual banter and camaraderie: coffee runs, locker room jokes, tobacco chewing, cigarette smoking, the quiet rhythm of small-unit trust—seemed to skip over Lester. He wasn't shunned outright, but there was a notable shift. A quiet one.

Everyone knew what he'd done—sending a rookie in alone—and though some "tacticians" might defend the move, the rank and file at Station 6 didn't. Their silence said enough. Rick could sense it. It was mildly tense for the next several days.

Rick, meanwhile, noticed a change of his own. The sideways glances turned into nods. Day after day, "Diaz" now became "Rick." That was the unspoken mark of belonging—the point where you weren't just wearing the badge, but had earned it. The station's rank and file no longer referred to Rick as a "rookie." Rick felt the sense of having earned an environment of belonging.

Lester and Rick did their daily walkthrough at the park. Lester would drive straight up Biscayne Boulevard, the same route, same time—same routine.

Rick dreaded it. It was because he was meticulous—borderline obsessive about his uniform and appearance. When he told Lou Ann she'd never see him with scuffed shoes, wrinkled pants, or a dull shine, he wasn't joking.

So, stepping out of the patrol car at 8:25 a.m., into the hot and humid air, walking through dew-soaked bushes, ducking under weaving spiderwebs, and tiptoeing across wet sand was Rick's daily personal nightmare. He moved like a man avoiding land mines—sidestepping leaves, weaving through branches, and watching every step for crab holes. All the while, he tried to keep his uniform immaculate as the balmy environment wrapped around him like a warm and wet towel. The air was still, heavy, and alive only with the hum of gnats and mosquitoes.

Rick always carried a hand towel in his Igloo lunch box with two bottles of water—one for drinking, one for cleanup. When they got back to the car, he'd blast the AC, soak the towel, and wipe down his face, arms, and finally, his shoes.

Lester always smirked, proud of the "Dirt Monster" nickname he'd earned crawling through this same swampy mess every morning. To Lester, this appeared to be his favorite part of the shift.

Rick questioned the point of it all. He had noticed the pattern—Lester's fixation on "consensual encounters" in the park, whether it was a prostitute or a homosexual relationship. Rick didn't say anything, but he knew this wasn't the kind of police work he wanted to model.

By week four, Rick had made up his mind. When he got his own assignment, there were two things he'd never do: harass a prostitute or do any drive-by or sweep of any park's bathroom. He didn't fancy Lester's *fetishes*.

And true to his words, once Rick was on his own—he never did either again.

VI
THE SOLO

It was Tuesday of week four when Sergeant Browne called Rick over to his office desk. Before getting there, Rick passed by and noted that the squad room was empty. The tone said it all—he was short on manpower.

"Diaz," Browne started, rubbing his temple, "I've got one on vacation, one on light duty who is stuck on the desk, one covering the strip, and Lester is in court this morning. That leaves me with three for the mainland zone. We're very shorthanded."

The Northeast District stretched west from Biscayne Bay to the I-95 and Turnpike, north to the Broward line at Golden Beach, and south to 125th Street. There was an east-west split clean down the middle by the Intracoastal at the Sunny Isles bridge.

"The strip," as everyone called it, covered the beach area—a small, polished stretch of low-rise, pastel-colored hotels, motels, souvenir stores, and retail shops that officers considered a prime patrol detail. Veteran officers loved to patrol there. The calls were light, the food was good, and the brass rarely showed face. It was the kind of tourist zone where cops had room to breathe, maybe even enjoy the shift, except during spring break when it got crazy. Drunk students, stupid fights, but cute girls.

Rick wouldn't mind working the strip that week, and Tony Roma's offered a free six-baby-back-rib meal to officers. *Sweet.* Even on a policeman's salary, dining at TR's was a relished, expensive treat.

Sergeant Browne leaned back in his chair, tapping a pen against the desk as if debating with himself before finally committing. "Want a cup of coffee?"

Rick responded, "I don't drink coffee, Sarge."

"All right, Diaz. Here's the deal. What I need...you're riding as a one-man unit today, at least until Lester gets back from court. Could be a few hours." He exhaled through his nose. "I already cleared it with Lieutenant Waters. We've *never* let a Phase 1 rookie ride solo, but he thinks you're good to go—and so do I. In your short time here, you've handled just about every dispatch call in the book. You think you can ride solo?"

Rick didn't flinch. "QSL, Sarge." He knew what this meant.

"Good. Lester is 6123 Alpha, you'll be 6123 Bravo." He's already in court." Browne tossed Rick a patrol car key. "That unit just came back from the motor pool. It's clean inside, but filthy outside. I wouldn't want to be seen driving it. You might want to hose it down before you roll out."

Rick's heart started pounding. *What the fuck?* Three weeks out of the academy, and now he was going solo—that was unheard of. A mix of adrenaline and disbelief overcame him.

He'd experience it twice, many years later, once when a senior law partner would tell Rick in a Miami courtroom, "*You're* lead on this trial. You know the case; you have ten minutes to do an opening statement outline. That's how I got thrown into the ring!"

And again, forty years later, as a private student pilot, when Rick's flight instructor would say, "Today, you're ready to do your first solo. I've already called the tower. The controller knows the situation. Listen to her—she'll guide you from the ground."

Different decades, different attire, same pulse, and each with its own type of danger.

Rick sat anxiously through three-officer roll call, the heel of his right foot nervously tapping on the floor. It was quick and businesslike, routine for all, except Rick.

"Sarge, who's playing temporary FTO for Lester's rookie?" a squad member asked.

"Nobody," Sergeant Browne said flatly.

While silence loomed, eyebrows raised among the small troop.

"The desk?"

"Nope," Sergeant Browne quipped, savoring the intrigue he created with his pause.

"He's solo until Lester gets back from court. He'll be 6123 Bravo. Lester checked in earlier as 6123 Alpha. You all keep an eye on Diaz."

The room remained silent for a moment. Browne made sure all knew that he had covered his ass, and continued, "I already cleared it with the lieutenant, and I called the communications commander. Dispatch knows the situation, and we need the coverage."

There was still a short pause and quiet looming.

"Look at you, kid!" one of the squad officers exclaimed. "No worries, we got your six. Just listen to the radio. Any uncertainty, say—'6121 to go to Channel D,' and I will walk you through it."

Rick tried to act unsurprised; he shrugged his shoulders as if saying, "Oh, well." He was really just disguising his extreme excitement. He kept his eyes forward, feeling all eyes on him.

Solo duty. Three weeks out of the academy. No partner. No immediate safety net.

"Rick, know your location at all times, you hear? And don't initiate anything you can't get yourself out of alone. Only take a signal if it's given to you. Clear?"

"Yes, sir."

As roll call broke, Rick felt the weight settle in. His heart was still beating so fast. Sergeant Browne's parting words hung in the air.

Rick was quick to leave the roll call, the chatter fading as the few remaining officers filtered out toward their units. He felt butterflies in his stomach—a restless energy he couldn't shake. The environment was quieter now, but the smell of coffee and cigarette smoke was still hanging in the air. Browne was still by the desk, flipping through papers on a clipboard, half-distracted.

Rick walked over. "Sarge?"

"Yeah?" Browne looked up from his clipboard.

"Today's my birthday," Rick said. "I have a birthday request."

Sergeant Browne raised an eyebrow. "You didn't ask for the day off?"

"I did—Lou Ann said we'd be short, so I withdrew it."

"So, what's the wish?" he asked.

Rick grinned. "I want to pull a prank on Lester."

Sergeant Browne's face tightened a fraction, then he smiled despite himself. "By doing what?"

"You know how he always runs that 10 at 170th and the Boulevard to sneak up on gay men in the park? I want to go on the radio as '6123 Bravo' and take a 10 at 170th with that QTH [location] as a one-man unit."

"That's wicked, Rick," he said, eyebrows lifting. "But love the idea. What the hell, he will get a kick out of it." A smirk crept in. "The troops will get a kick out of the rookie throwing a jab at his FTO."

"And even after that fake 10, wait until Lester's back in the zone, and don't get into anything you can't get yourself out of."

As Rick hurried down the hallway, his excitement evidenced by the vibrating in his steps, he pushed open the rear door—and froze. Standing there was Kojak.

"Morning, sir," Rick said, stepping past him, looking for the numbered patrol car matching the number on the key chain.

"Whoa! Come back here!" Waters called.

Rick paused.

"You don't need to salute me, but you should address me as 'Lieutenant,' okay? You're doing very well so far, but don't forget, you're still a rookie."

As he continued to walk out of the station, Rick quickly muttered, "Sorry, Lieutenant. Won't happen again!"

Waters called after him, shaking his head. "Wait, wait, wait...I'm not through! Where's the fire? What's the rush?"

Rick glanced back, feeling the tension mixed with exhilaration.

The lieutenant's voice softened. "Listen, kid, I know you're excited to solo. Who wouldn't be? But come on inside. Let's talk for a minute."

Is this really necessary? Rick thought to himself. He turned around and adjusted his pace. It felt like being held at your bedroom door by a parent on Christmas morning, waiting to look under the tree.

Lieutenant Waters led Rick to the office marked with a placard: *Lieutenant's Office*. "Have a seat. The coffee is fresh, and it's good—not that department-purchased garbage. I buy it, I bring it, I hide it. And I don't invite many to it. Help yourself."

"Thanks, but I don't drink coffee, Lieutenant," Rick replied.

Waters smiled at Rick. "I've heard that from other rookies before. Well, you will someday. Wait till you go to mids!" He chuckled. He then reached into his drawer, pulled out a can of Skoal, and asked casually, "Do you dip?"

Rick blinked. He had no idea what that work meant. At first, Rick thought dipping was some type of ballroom dance and laughed respectfully at his question.

Waters raised an eyebrow. "It's a tobacco thing."

"Chewing tobacco?" Rick asked cautiously.

"No, it's like chewing tobacco, but less nasty. Don't let any motherfucker get you started on either. It's an addiction."

Rick understood this was all part of an exercise—an intentional way to slow him down, to ease him into his first solo shift. Nothing more. So yes, it *was* necessary.

"Patrol means to drive slowly and scan," Waters continued, his tone firm but calm. "You can't see crime or suspicious activity if you're at or above the speed limit. The slower you drive, the more you will detect, and the better cop you'll be. Lester will be back by noon. Just be careful out there."

Back then, *Hill Street Blues* was a very popular police show on television—seventeen years before the internet changed everything. It had a visceral feeling to it, and a uniformed patrol squad sergeant, Phil Esterhaus, whose morning roll-call sendoff became a national mantra:

Let's be careful out there.

Those words echoed through departments across the country—and they still do today, decades later. Unlike earlier cop shows, *Hill Street Blues* felt more like a reality series, a gritty approximation of life in the high-crime major city, as real as Hollywood could make it. Suspension of disbelief was unnecessary, as it was so authentic.

There was a certain musical theme leading into the introduction scene of each episode that made the viewer want to be there. Hearing it from the lieutenant made it raw and real as it rang with unexpected warmth.

Rick absorbed the lieutenant's words, catching both the direct instruction and the warning: *Go slow.*

"You are excused, Diaz."

Despite Waters's pep talk, Rick couldn't help the bounce in his pace as he spotted the unit waiting for him—a beat-up patrol car sitting in the lot like a girl showing up to a first date without makeup or polished nails.

As he got closer, Rick realized that the unit wasn't just rough around the edges. She was downright and embarrassingly filthy, and no garden hose could cosmetically make her up.

When Rick checked in as "6-1-2-3 Bravo," all officers monitoring the district's radio channel were perplexed. It was unheard of that a three-week rookie would go solo. Jokes were made of women being big gossipers, but truth be told, cops were way worse.

The marked patrol unit needed real elbow grease, not just a rinse. Rick wasn't about to roll up his sleeves and scrub it himself to sweat and dirty his uniform. So, he took it through a nearby automatic wash—on his own dime, which he gladly paid without hesitation.

When the unit rolled out of the port with the grime now stripped away, he felt a quiet surge of pride. His uniform and his unit bore a notable luster. For a moment, he might as well have been a peacock. Another small, private victory.

If only my mom could see me now, Rick thought.

VII
THE NEXT PHASE

Rick drove out north to the Boulevard, cruising close to the park. When the radio traffic was silent, he clicked the mic.

"Six-one-two-three Bravo. Show me one-man, 09, and then show me on a 10 at 170th and the Boulevard, northbound for an area check of the men's bathroom at the park."

Silence followed—then came the chorus of *click, click, click, click, click* over the police radio. That had a particular meaning, the equivalent of a vivid outburst of laughter.

Every officer listening knew exactly what those clicks meant: contagious laughter. Rick's little stunt had just gone district-wide—viral. He was clearly taking a playful jab at Lester, and everyone caught it instantly.

In the station, Lieutenant Waters burst into the sergeant's office. "Ed, what the fuck is the rookie doing taking a signal 10 at the park? Didn't you tell him—"

"Relax, Jimmy," Sergeant Browne interrupted, leaning in toward the radio. "Listen up...here it comes."

The dispatcher's voice cut in: "Six-one-two-three Bravo, you said you were a one-man unit?"

Rick paused, then said, "QSL," trying to contain his chuckle as he savored the setup. What he was about to say would echo through the station all day.

"Six-one-two-three...oh-seven. Access too difficult."

The radio now exploded with another wave of clicks—dozens this time.

Waters slapped the desk and laughed. "Fucking Cuban rookie! That kid's got some wit and big balls. Shots fired hot at his FTO."

"Yeah," Browne said, grinning. "You know, John, I got a special request from FTO Farina to take Diaz for Phase 2. What do you think?"

"Bad idea. Farina won't engage. He's afraid to do anything proactive right now."

"I know, but he's the district's best FTO. The kid's had enough for a while since the robbery. Vince can still teach him well. I think it's a good fit for both of them. The rookie's energy and enthusiasm might do Vince some good and vice versa—it will put some mustard on that hot dog, Diaz. You agree?"

"Point well taken, yep. Do it," Browne joined.

Everybody wondered whether Lester heard Diaz's prank, as he was in court, but it didn't matter. Rick's prank now made him somewhat of a born legend among the entire shift platoon.

Lunch hour rolled around, and Rick stuck to his ritual—a homemade tuna fish salad sandwich. He had perfected the recipe: fresh Wonder Bread, Bumble Bee albacore tuna, a touch of relish, red onion, mustard, mayo, a squeeze of lemon, salt, pepper, and the secret ingredient—a pinch of sugar. Alongside it, a carrot, two celery sticks, a green apple, and, as always, two bottles of water and one of orange juice. The lunch menu was the same, five days a week.

Today, he was having lunch alone, as Lester was still delayed in court.

Despite his luscious sandwich, Rick wanted ever so badly to take a 12—the radio code for lunch—and head over to the Rascal House restaurant to see the waitress he'd been eyeing for weeks. "Pretty" wasn't the right word. She was stunning—bright, dimpled smile; great skin; perfectly aligned with white teeth; pronounced rosy cheeks; an easy laugh; and just enough confidence in herself, despite her little apron, to make him lose his train of thought every time she asked, "Refill?"

It was a bit out of his assigned zone, but everyone crossed that imaginary line now and then. And Red had invited Rick to do so earlier; Rick had his "blessing." Diner-type food was great, and cops got 50 percent off.

Still, Rick knew better. The risk was too great. Orders were orders, and his word was—and had always been—his bond.

So, at noon sharp, Rick instead drove to the park. Not to spy on potential homosexual behavior, but instead to enjoy his brief lunch in *peace*—shade overhead, birds chirping, squirrels darting through the trees. He parked under a live oak, killed the running engine, and unwrapped his sandwich like it was a ceremonial picnic.

As he chewed and monitored the police radio, he caught sight of something familiar—two cars parked by the men's restroom. One man exited, heading toward his vehicle. The other one was vacant. Even from a distance, Rick could see it: that unmistakable shift from satisfaction to sudden fear the moment they noticed his patrol car, and Rick just couldn't help himself.

He flipped on his overhead lights and gave the siren a quick *chirp*. Both men froze, glanced at him, and hurried to their respective cars. Rick smiled to himself, took another bite of his sandwich, and thought, *Lester would've loved that one.*

Rick got on his loudspeaker. "Don't worry, I'm on my lunch break; your secret is safe with me." He was a nice guy, but he could be a cynical, comical asshole given the right circumstances.

As soon as Rick sank his teeth into the sandwich, the radio broke its silence.

"Six-one-two-three Alpha, show me 09," Lester's deep voice keyed in, announcing that he was back in the district from his downtown court appearance.

The dispatcher came right back: "Six-one-two-three Alpha, QSK."

"Six-one-two-three Alpha—have 6123 Bravo 05 to the station to meet up." Before the dispatcher could call Rick on the radio, another voice cut in.

"Six-one-two-three," Sergeant Browne's tone cracked through the static. "Have 6123 Alpha and Bravo switch to Channel D."

Click. Silence. Then another *click.*

All three were now on Channel D—a restricted frequency not open to the public, though every cop in the district knew they could flip the radio on, dial, and listen in and not be detected. Each click over meant another officer had joined on the channel, but you could never tell who or how many unless they identified themselves by speaking on the Channel D radio frequency.

Every curious officer in the district switched their channel. The air filled with soft static and unspoken curiosity. Nobody said a word, but almost every ear was listening.

Finally, Browne's voice returned, measured but firm. "Lester, you stay one-man as Alpha for the remainder. Diaz, remain 6123 Bravo. See you both at the station at 06 time."

"Oh-six" marked the end-of-shift sign-off—the only part of the night that many times never came on time.

"QSL," both officers answered in near unison.

When they switched back to the main channel, the radio fell quiet again—just the low hum of traffic and the occasional dispatch call.

Sergeant Browne keyed up once more, this time for the dispatcher. "Dispatch, treat 6123 Alpha and Bravo as *two* one-man units. Copy?"

"QSL 6120," the dispatcher replied—*message understood.*

The message was clear. Everybody, including Rick, knew exactly what that meant. Rick was good enough to be solo, a signal that they could count on him.

Were Diaz and Lester at odds? Was someone in trouble? The answer was neither—but the curiosity lingered, and it was the buzz of the day and for some more thereafter.

But the next day, Sergeant Browne paired Lester and Rick again. Between them, things were good, or at least good enough, but the troops suspected otherwise.

Privately, Sergeant Browne told Rick he thought he was ready to be cut loose; that Rick didn't need to go through Phases 2 and 3—but not doing so would be unprecedented.

Rick understood. He was hoping instead to ride with Farina.

A week later, Lester signed off on Rick's Phase 1 evaluation—excellent in every category: appearance, punctuality, courtesy, procedures, knowledge of the law, situational awareness, writing, and radio handling. Every box was checked all the way to the right, top to bottom. Rick passed with distinction.

Now Phase 2—the morning shift, 7:00 a.m. to 3:00 p.m.—a different zone entirely. Norland, low-income housing projects, and a cluster of banks and easy-target gas stations that seemed to invite trouble. The income level here was one-quarter of Aventura's, and crime was more than double.

What Rick didn't know was that his new training officer, Farina, was under investigation at the time. The incident involved several MDPD officers and a man named Nathan Flower.

The three officers had a valid search warrant—wrong house, though. A struggle broke out, and Flower got the worse end of the fight and ended up in the hospital with serious head injuries. Word around the station was that a few cops—including Farina—might be indicted. Still, Farina had clout at Station 6. He kept his FTO status and asked to take Rick through Phase 2, and his wish was granted. The 5 percent pay bump for training a rookie didn't hurt either.

The 7:00 a.m. roll call wrapped up. As the room emptied, Farina turned to Rick. "Did Lester ever let you drive?"

"No."

"What a dick." Farina tossed the keys across the table. "You drive."

Vince Farina was Rick's idol—fit, polished, tactical. The real deal. Rick admired that. He was fascinated by Vietnam—and very angry about it—it took his best friend at age ten. His father had served in the Army, and that made Rick a real patriot.

But there was another reason Rick was attracted to Vietnam. Every evening in the 1960s, he'd sit glued to the television, watching Walter Cronkite describe the day's events in the war. The footage was real—raw. The body climbed every night; Rick kept count.

When Rick was ten years old, his neighbor Stevie Gomez, eight years older but like a big brother, was drafted into the Army. The day before he shipped out to Vietnam, Stevie came over after hearing that Rick cried over getting the news.

After all, a year earlier, Rick had already lost another friend, Cliffy Knapp, in the 1969 DC-4 cargo plane crash on Northwest 36th Street in Miami. At the young age of ten, Rick understood the unforeseeable death of an all-too-young and closest friend.

Stevie jumped over the fence that separated the Gomezes' house from the Diazes' house. He kneeled down to meet Rick's eyes. "Ricky, I'm coming home after a tour. It's only six months, like a long summer. I will be back."

They hugged—long and tight. Stevie let go first, then Rick, remembering Cliffy.

"Look at me," Stevie said.

Rick raised his head slowly. Their eyes locked.

Stevie gripped both of Rick's shoulders, gave him a small shake, and said, "I will be back, I promise." Then he stood, turned, hopped the fence to his own yard, and disappeared inside his house.

Rick would never see Stevie again.

A week before he was supposed to come back from leave, a mortar round caught him in the back and ended everything in an instant.

Just another American boy KIA. His parents, Stevie Sr. and Olga, immediately sold their home, moved away, and were never seen or heard from thereafter. Grief hollowed them out, and they slipped quietly out of everyone's world. No forwarding address. No word since.

To this day, Stevie's name rests in the long curve of the Vietnam Veterans Memorial in Washington, DC—cold stone, carved letters, the only place his name still stands. He'd made sergeant just before he died—at a mere eighteen years old.

Every time Rick visits Washington, DC, he stops by the memorial, looks up the index names of G, then glosses down to "Gomez," then, taking a ritualistic deep breath, looks further down until arriving at "Steve." And every time, without fail, tears fall. He lets them. It's the last part of Stevie he still gets to carry—a deep childhood, life-lasting memory.

Maybe that was why, when Rick looked at Farina, something unspoken immediately connected Rick to him. There was a warm sense of connective familiarity.

They checked in with Dispatch and rolled out. It was an early morning, and the radio was unsurprisingly quiet.

As they reached their patrol area, Rick asked, "Anywhere in particular?"

"Yeah—199th and Northwest 2nd Avenue."

"The Ranch House?" Rick asked hopefully.

Farina smirked. "Over there, it's either the strip club or the Ranch House, and it's 7:45 a.m.—coffee time, what do you think?"

Rick grinned, pulse quickening. Could there be a pretty waitress there, too?

"Um. Are we having breakfast?"

"Nope," Farina said, adjusting his mirrored sunglasses. "Just coffee. Best in the zone. Pretty waitresses, too."

"By the way, and speaking of pretty girls," Farina said as they cruised north on 2nd Avenue, "Lou Ann asked me to ask you something."

Rick glanced over, suspicious. "Yeah? What's that?"

"She wants to know if you've got a girlfriend."

Rick shook his head, smiling faintly.

"I mean, hell, I can't believe she's got her eye on you," Farina went on. "I'm not saying she's old enough to be your mother, but she's what—thirty-two, thirty-three? Divorced, too, and from what I heard, it was ugly. She's on the rebound —not good."

"Jesus, Vince," Rick said. "She wants me to meet her daughter. Probably afraid she's gonna end up with the wrong type of guy. Must've had her young—sixteen, seventeen maybe." His voice trailed off. He stayed quiet. Red had already warned him.

"Well?" Farina pressed. "You got a girlfriend or not?"

"No," Rick said finally. "I date whoever I want, whenever I want."

Farina laughed. "Oh, excuse me, Don Julio!"

"Julio" was a term cops tossed around for Cubans.

"No, Vince—it's not like that," Rick said. "I don't have a *girlfriend*. I date several different girls depending on what I want to do and who's interested and available."

"So, you *are* a Don Julio," Farina teased.

"Fuck, man, you don't get it," Rick said, laughing now. "One girl loves bowling—so if I feel like bowling, I call her. Another likes fishing, another fine dining. I pick what I want to do, then I match the girl. Some love disco dancing—ha!"

Farina grinned, shaking his head. "All right, then, it's settled. Your call sign will be either 'Don Julio' or 'Saturday Night Rick'—take your pick."

They parked and walked into the Ranch House. No pretty waitress was visible, at least not yet. But the morning was young, and he was feeling lucky.

"Two coffees, please—black for me," Farina said to the woman behind the counter.

"Only one," Rick added.

Vince raised an eyebrow. "No coffee?"

"I don't drink coffee." Rick paused, looking around the room. "Vince, can I ask you something about the offices in this district?"

"Shoot."

Rick leaned back in the booth, eyes moving from one table to the next. "I feel like I'm physically in Miami but living in some small Western town. Almost all the officers here smoke, chew, or 'dip'—whatever the fuck *that* means—and they all drink their coffee black. They've got Southern accents that somehow sound Western, and most have a mustache. They all look like the Marlboro Man—just missing the Stetson hat, the Jensen boots, and a horse."

Vince had just taken a sip of his coffee when the words hit him. Before he could enjoy his sip, he sprayed it across the table and onto Rick's shirt. He tried to apologize, but he couldn't control his teary-eyed laughter that went on for a while.

Rick sat still for a second, eyes closed, coffee dripping down his chin and onto his shirt. He wiped himself off with a napkin, muttering, "Glad you found that funny."

Vince was still catching his breath. "Jesus, Rick—you're right. I've just become immune to it all."

Rick smirked, blotting the last of the mess off his shirt. "I just call it like I see it."

All of a sudden, a pretty waitress came out from the kitchen, as attractive as the cute one at the Rascal House. A perfect touch of makeup caught the low light. Rick did not want to meet her covered in coffee, but there was no avoiding her—it was too late.

She walked straight up to Rick, pulled a clean napkin from her apron, wet it with a pitcher of water, and handed it to him.

"Did you burn yourself with your coffee, officer?"

"Yes—I mean, no."

"Well, which is it?"

"Yes, it burns a little. And no, it wasn't my coffee—it was his." Rick nodded toward Vince. "I don't drink coffee."

She smiled. "Well, you don't know what you're missing."

"Oh, I know, everyone around here tells me it's the best coffee around," Rick replied, half-grinning.

"Speaking of missing," she said, tilting her head, "you missed some spots. May I?"

Rick froze. Embarrassed and oddly deflated, he surrendered. "Sure."

She stepped closer, dabbing gently at his cheek, then his jaw. Her perfume lingered—something floral but clean, like spring air after rain. Inexpensive, but not cheap. She bent slightly, close enough for him to smell her perfume, and view her cleavage—and he sure did.

Then came the final two dabs—light, teasing, straight across his upper and lower lips.

"There ya go," she said softly as she drew back in a mildly sexy way, staring him in the eyes during this seductive exercise. "Good as new. Speaking of new—*you* look new."

Rick hesitated but saw the answer as not only a propriety but an opportunity. "I am."

"How new?"

"One month."

"That's as new as it gets." She smiled, started to turn away, then paused. "What's your name?"

"Rick."

Her eyes switched to his nameplate. "Your last name says 'Diaz.' Cuban?" She pronounced it perfectly.

"Yes, I'm Cuban American," Rick said, offering a small smile, hoping it would interest her, fearing it would not.

"*Cubanito bonito*," she said, grinning with a flash of warmth and mischief, before turning to walk back to the counter, piercing the table's 100 percent discounted check through the spindle, and leaving Rick with a flutter of anticipation.

Vince leaned back in the booth and stretched both arms across the backrest before returning to stir and enjoy the last of his rich, aromatic coffee with the end of his spoon. "Ha! I was right—you are a Don Julio. Take her out to a Saturday-night disco; she can be your next dancing date."

Rick remained silent—not a bad idea, but a bit too early.

"All kidding aside, she's cute," Vince said, nodding toward the counter. "And she likes you."

Rick smirked and said nothing, but the thought was already well in motion.

"But listen—Lou Ann's daughter?" Vince continued, lowering his voice. "That's a mistake. Stay away from that."

Rick nodded affirmatively. The tone had shifted; this wasn't teasing anymore.

"Anyway," Vince said, straightening up, "now, your real call sign." He paused for effect, letting it hang in the air. "Defender."

Rick raised an eyebrow. "*Defender?*"

"Yeah. It fits." Vince leaned in, his voice dropping again, the gruffness giving way to something almost paternal. "It's early, but we don't see many recruits like you. You've got good basic instincts and great writing skills. You've got balls. You just need someone to show you how not to fuck up, and that's me!"

The problem, though, was that with the investigation looming, Vince did not want to do anything proactive. He didn't know that Rick already knew about it. He must have been embarrassed to reveal it to Rick.

And now Rick knew that the lack of proactiveness was just putting action on hold, but he'd learn so much more from this Vietnam vet who seemed to relish the relationship. It was almost as if he were fatalistic that the outcome of the investigation might make Rick his last rookie trainee, and he had one with whom he thought his teachings might matter, sort of like an anticipatory reward to his potential fate.

He sat back again and tapped his mug. "Now, about that waitress—if you decide to go for it, remember something: She takes *good* care of us. If a cop breaks her heart, she might start charging the rest of us. We get 50 percent off at most places in the district. Red's well-liked. But *here?*" He pointed a finger at the table. "Here we pay *nothing* for coffee and 50 percent on any meal. So always leave a nice tip."

He looked Rick dead in the eye. "And don't fuck that up."

Exiting the Ranch House, they stopped just outside the double entrance doors at a newspaper stand.

Vince popped a quarter into the slot, pulled out a copy of *The Miami Herald*, and nodded toward the unit. "Drive to Miami Gardens Drive and stop under the overpass, in the shade, and back it in, all the way to the wall so we can't get ambushed from behind."

Rick knew then and there that Vince was not only a street-savvy cop, but also still carried his Vietnam life into the police car.

Rick got there quickly and tucked the unit under the I-95 overpass.

Vince unfolded the paper, leaning back as if time didn't matter. He read it slowly, methodically, like a man scanning more than the headlines.

An hour passed. Quiet radio traffic, no calls.

Finally, he folded the paper, looked up, and said simply, "New QTH. Drive toward the train tracks and make a right just before them."

The next stop was a small, tired-looking shopping plaza. "Barbershop," Vince said.

Rick was curious but followed as he was told and headed toward the red-white-and-blue rotating barber's pole. Above, a sign read *Frankie's Barbershop*.

As soon as they stepped inside, a man with a thick New Jersey–Italian accent lit up. "Vinny! Where ya been? We miss ya! How's da court case goin'?"

Vince's smile faltered, just for a second. "Good, Frankie," he said flatly, immediately changing the subject. He climbed into the barber's chair and got a quick cut and a clean shave while they talked about everything *except* the case.

Rick remained attentive to his handheld radio.

When he was done, the barber turned to Rick. "This your new rookie?"

"Yep," Vince said.

"Hey, kid," the barber grinned, "you want a cleanup? No charge—it's on the house."

Rick was told to stay away from gratuities—except at mealtime, whether the Rascal House, the Ranch House, or anywhere else, for that matter. Free or discounted coffee and meals were just a part of police-public relations back then.

"Thanks, but it's still short enough—just got a cut a few days ago," Rick said, escaping the appearance of rudely rejecting the courtesy.

As they pulled away from the barber shop, Vince finally broke the silence. "If you ever scrape your unit and it's nothing major, swing by here. He's got the exact green-and-white color-matched paint, will fix it clean and fast. Saves you a pile of paperwork—and a 'preventable accident' on your record. No charge. Slip him a twenty."

Rick nodded but didn't answer. He wasn't sure if this was some kind of test or just Vince being...*Vince*.

They left, and Vince gave Rick another QTH. This time, it was an auto body shop—also owned by an Italian guy, but this one really looked the part. He was Sicilian. Slick hair, gold chain, diamond pinky ring—the whole wiseguy aesthetic.

Vince nodded toward Rick. "Giuseppe, you see this kid's face? You take care of him, like he's me."

The man smiled broadly, gripping Rick's hand. "Always, Vince. For you—the world."

Vince was no cowboy and didn't chew tobacco or smoke cigarettes. He didn't fit the general mold of the district, but now it seemed like he was *the* Italian connection. Rick was certain that when lunch time rolled around, it'd be Italian, too.

Rick was a bit lost but now seemed to understand Vince's predicament. Four hours into the shift, and they hadn't done a damn thing. No calls. No reports. Just aimless driving and personalized random stops that made no "police sense."

Rick eventually pieced it together. Word around the station was that Vince was under investigation—a serious one, and the State Attorney's Office was under pressure from community groups to bring charges. Vince was playing it low and slow, doing only what was assigned. No self-initiated stops. No risks.

Then, suddenly and without warning, Vince made a hard right turn, then another, circling through side streets until they came to an abrupt stop in the middle of a quiet neighborhood.

"Close your eyes," he said flatly.

Rick hesitated. "Sir?"

"I said *close your eyes*."

Rick instantly obeyed.

Seconds ticked by. Then Vince's voice cut through the silence.

"Exactly where are we?"

Rick opened his eyes, caught off guard. "We're around—"

"*Around?*" Vince's voice rose, sharp. "*Around* ain't good enough. You need to know exactly where you are—*always*. Lester didn't teach you that shit, did he?"

Rick shook his head. "No, sir."

"He should've," Vince muttered. He shifted in his seat, his tone lowered, almost confessional. "I've got a situation that forces me to lay low. I can't afford to make mistakes. I don't initiate shit, as you have seen, but there's still a lot I can teach you."

He threw the car into gear, eyes fixed ahead. "Let's get lunch. Go to Mario's on Dixie Highway and 127th Street. Best lasagna in town and awesome garlic rolls. Keep this to yourself, but when Sammy is there, it's not even 'point five'—it's all free."

Another "Italian connection," Rick thought.

No pretty waitresses at Mario's, but Rick gladly traded free Italian meals for his delicious but laboriously homemade tuna salad sandwiches. He would compensate for it in the gym.

"Okay, Rick, good day. Let's head to the barn."

The engine rumbled as they pulled away. The "barn" was the nickname for Station 6.

By the end of the shift, they'd done zero proactive work—no stats, just another day on patrol. This pattern repeated for weeks. Each shift felt identical, but Vince still taught Rick something new every day. He just wouldn't engage, and it didn't matter.

Rick understood.

By their third week together, breaking news hit: The state attorney announced that all involved officers were cleared.

There were a few street protests, critics on some radio shows, a small crowd of objectors shouting and holding poster signs outside the courthouse, but nothing that got out of hand. The city exhaled—cautiously.

The next shift felt different from the start. Vince's posture was suddenly lighter; he was more animated and talkative. As they pulled out of Station 6, Rick reached for the radio to check in, but Vince's hand shot out, intercepting it.

"Six-one-one-two," Vince said, steady. "Two officers, 09, and show us on a 19—north on the Boulevard. Florida plate ADC 756, one occupant."

This was the huge moment Vinny had been waiting for, apparently for over a year now.

The radio clicked instantly—*click, click, click*. Static filled the air, heavy with celebration. It wasn't just a call—it was a resounding statement. Vince was *back*.

As they approached the car, Vince unholstered and held his weapon low at his side, out of the driver's sight. The car's windows were blacked out. Vince probed the trunk, as Keith had done six months earlier on the ride-along. Vince exchanged a few quiet words with the driver, then waved him off.

Back in the patrol unit, the silence lingered.

"Rick," Vince finally said, his voice low but sharp. "Why didn't you draw your weapon when I did?"

"I thought it was a routine traffic stop," Rick answered. "In the academy, we were trained to stay holstered if it is only a traffic stop."

"Fuck the academy!" Vince snapped. "If we could have seen inside, maybe no need to have it out. But we couldn't."

Rick stammered. "I hear you. It's just—"

"There's nothing routine about any traffic stop," Vince shot back. "And I'm not telling you to pull your gun on everyone every time, either—but when in doubt, pull it out. We couldn't see who was inside or what they were doing. Got me? I'm going home tonight, how about you? Fuck the unknown civilian until you are certain he's QRU. The driver had no idea I was target-ready. And if he did and made a complaint, so be it."

The lesson was clear.

A week later, Vince signed Rick off for his third and final FTO phase. It was also shift-rotation time, which meant that certain squad officers would be leaving and others coming in.

"We're throwing a squad party," Vince said. "Rookies don't get invited—but *you're* in. It's a pool party. Everyone's bringing a girlfriend or wife." He smirked. "Why don't you invite that waitress from the Ranch House? We all know her."

Rick gave him a polite smile but said nothing.

He showed up to the party alone, except with a hot pot of his mom's secret recipe of black beans and rice. It was a huge hit.

Vince laughed: "No sucking up here; you're welcome to do that again anytime."

Rick was now *on the team.*

Phase 3 was uneventful—a polish on the edges left from the earlier two FTOs. Rick was eager to get "cut loose"—the ultimate solo.

There was one Black female officer on his third FTO squad. Her name was Katherine McGruder, and she took to Rick from day one. She was around thirty, with a face like Tina Turner—same smile, same fire—but without the height or thunder thighs. She was sharp, outspoken, and unapologetically protective.

"You're smart," she told Rick once. "And don't let this place make you dumb. Continue your education; use the tuition referral program—you could be director one day." She covered him like a helicopter sister.

When he finally passed all three phases, Rick was officially "cut loose." He miraculously escaped the graveyard shift, which was no small victory. It never happened to a rookie. But Red had made it clear: Diaz was too valuable for midnights. Rick wasn't favored; the district just had a bigger need for a Spanish speaker on days and afternoons. With no mids, Rick was still not a coffee drinker.

Midnights sucked. Everyone knew it. It was only for rookies, officers who had a secondary day job, and newly promoted supervisors.

Rick didn't argue with the blessing. Five years living in Spain had left his Spanish flawless, and the thought of avoiding the midnight grind was like winning the lottery.

VIII
THE CLASSROOM

While still a rookie but still on probation, Rick went on to become an FTO himself and was sent to a wide array of specialized training schools: advanced self-defense, VIP and dignitary protection, Secret Service training, DEA investigator school, Professor Techniques Workshop, and Interview and Interrogation courses, among others.

In 1981, Rick was invited to three detective bureaus: Robbery, Homicide, and the elite Organized Crime Bureau (OCB). Narcotics, vice, intelligence, money-laundering.

In the next four years, Rick was primarily an "undercover narc," just in time to parallel his new assignment to Miami Vice. He joined Florida's Vice-Presidential Drug Task Force Group and made major drug seizures and forfeitures. Not enough for Rick.

As soon as he was eligible to test for sergeant, Rick took the written examination—and he scored at the very top among nearly 200 candidates. The problem: That year, due to a discrimination lawsuit, promotions were no longer based on an objective written test, and only 33 percent of that result counted toward the promotion, with the rest determined by a subjective Assessment Center, a panel review of practical scenarios, adjusted by seniority points.

There was no coincidence in the obvious pattern on the list that followed: Within every group of ten candidates, there were about four males—two Black, two white; four females—two Black, two white; and two Hispanics—mainly males, since back then there were few Hispanic females with PSD, by then renamed as Metro Police.

Decades later, you could sprinkle in an occasional Asian and Haitian. Bottom line: Rick dropped far down the list, and when the few positions were filled, he didn't make the cut, dying high on the promotions list. That defeat defined a change in his career path—a blessing in disguise.

Not making sergeant hit Rick harder than anything in his life. He wasn't used to falling short—of anything. The only blow that could have cut deeper would've been losing the badge altogether. He'd been the highest-scoring Hispanic candidate on the written test, but the Assessment Center had little to do with merit and everything to do with getting veteran offices promoted, shielding the city from civil liability, and appeasing truly unqualified minorities. If that was not quota-based, nothing was.

The setback didn't come alone. Two more shoot-outs, the pressure to earn a much better living, and a chance conversation with a judge all collided into a single truth Rick could no longer ignore: He should consider a career change.

But what, where, and how?

In 1984, a Miami-Dade Circuit Court judge invited Rick into his chambers during an OCB case trial right after Rick testified and said, "Detective, I've now seen you testify twice in my courtroom—both drug trafficking and money laundering trials. How far did you go in school?"

"I have two associate degrees, Your Honor," Rick answered.

"Go to law school," the judge told him. "You're wasted on what your department pays. You'd be a better lawyer."

He paused, studying Rick with a sharp, almost knowing look. "Do you know what I did before I ever put on this robe?"

Rick thought for a moment. "A lawyer?"

"Yes," the judge said with a nod. "But before that?"

Rick shook his head side to side. "No."

"A motorcycle officer for the City of Miami," the judge said.

That was all Rick needed. Rick's disappointment morphed into furious motivation. It's amazing how some random thing one person said could inspire such life-changing decisions.

Rick took out loans and made full advantage of his department's education/tuition-reimbursement program. He earned his bachelor's degree in six months—doing regular courses, mini-masters, summer sessions—and received twenty-seven lifetime credits for his five years of service with the department.

Before his graduation, Rick signed up for the LSAT. He took it—and scored embarrassingly low, despite holding a 4.0 GPA. He applied to the only law school that might accept him: St. Thomas University College of Law in Miami. It was in its charter year—unaccredited at the time, private, expensive, but hunting for students willing to chance the risk or those not good enough to gain acceptance elsewhere. Out-of-state applicants were virtually nonexistent. Even for locals, it was a huge gamble. Rick didn't apply anywhere else. He needed to stay local, and the other accredited law school would never admit him. He'd stay working for the department and go to law school full time.

Rick passed the preliminary application process and

received an invitation for an interview. The then-dean, Alan Waltz, greeted him in his second-floor office.

After the pleasantries, the dean asked bluntly: "Why does a student with a 4.0 GPA do so poorly on the LSAT? You have the lowest score I've ever seen!"

Rick explained, "I didn't have the time or money for the prep course sir—it's $800. I worked the midnight shift the night before the test and went straight to the test center."

"Well, that explains it. So, tell me—why do you want to be a lawyer, and why here? Why this school?"

"I have no shot anywhere else, sir. I help support my parents, so I must stay here. No school will take me with that LSAT score. I can't leave Miami; I need to keep my secure job. And I have it now, with the Metro Police Department. If I resign and this school doesn't get accredited, I'm—*frankly*—fucked."

"So, how will you do it?" the dean asked.

"I'll work mids, 10:00 p.m. to 6:00 a.m., and catch up on sleep on weekends," Rick replied.

"You're nuts," Waltz said, with a laugh, "but if you're gambling on us, we're gambling on you. You've got maturity, mentality, hunger, and your GPA tells me you'll make it. Congrats. Registration's next week. What area do you patrol?"

"This one, sir."

Waltz lifted his brows. "No kidding? So, you defend this campus?"

"Yup."

"How long you been on?" Waltz asked.

"Five years, sir."

"I'm sure you've seen a lot," he added.

Rick hesitated, weighing what he was willing to open up. "I have, and I'm ready to move on to another professional life," he said finally, keeping his tone flat.

Waltz didn't push. He didn't have to; Rick's silence had spoken for itself, and loudly.

Days passed in a blur of preparation, paperwork, and personal adjustments.

Rick prepared for his exit from OCB; he'd go back to Uniform Patrol on mids with weekends off. He met with the Northwest District major—Juan Gonzalez—and asked if he'd take Rick in a swap. He agreed.

Rick expressed his need to study, so Gonzalez said, "I will make you OIC [Officer in Charge], Midnight Platoon, and you can work in the station on the front desk. No officer senior to you can bump you. I don't want to receive a single complaint against you or it's off; I don't care if you study or read *Playboy* magazines. You want Fridays and Saturdays off? You got it!"

Rick turned in his transfer request, and his wish was granted. No promotion to sergeant with a gold badge or chevron stripes.

This was a small step backward to later take leaps and bounds forward. Rick's gamble would pay off huge. He just needed to graduate from law school, and, of course, there was the accreditation. But that was out of his hands.

On the first day of class, the lobby at St. Thomas was buzzing well before the official 8:00 a.m. start. Everyone had arrived early, eager and anxious.

"Look at the roster," a school official called out. "Every name has an *A* or *B* next to it. This line is for the *A*'s. This other line is for—?"

A wave of silence followed.

"Y'all too tight or too nervous! It's *B*. Yes, *B*! And none of y'all better be signing up to go on *Jeopardy*."

A ripple of laughter ran through the breezeway. The official's humor eased the tension, giving everyone a moment to breathe.

"Vince! What the hell?"

"Rick! No, it can't be! You coming here?"

"No, I'm working an undercover job, and you just blew my cover..."

Rick froze for a split second, caught off guard by seeing a fellow officer in such an unexpected setting. Vince hesitated, too, unsure if he should say anything in front of the others for Rick's sake. For a few seconds, they just stared at each other, the room buzzing around them, everyone pretending not to notice.

"Just kidding, Vince. I'm not in OCB anymore."

Overwhelmed by the encounter, Rick bumped Vince lightly with an elbow in a familiar, friendly way.

"What section are you in, A or B?" Vince asked, still grinning.

"A," Rick replied. "You?"

"A, too!" Vince said, laughing. "Holy shit—law school partners. Three years! Amazing."

Rick shook his head, still processing the coincidence. "Wait, Vince. We need to talk. What unit are you in?"

"None," Vince said flatly. "I retired."

"What? When? Why?" Rick's eyes widened, his voice a mix of shock and disbelief.

"You didn't hear?"

"No!"

"I was in a foot chase...busted my kneecap real bad. The county gave me a workers' comp washout. Got a good chunk of money. Here I am. You?"

"Still working," Rick said. "Northwest mids—the front desk."

"You're nuts," Vince said, half-laughing. "No leave?"

"I tried," Rick said, shaking his head. "The director called me in. Said that I was too valuable to let go; that I was a huge asset to OCB; that I was seizing and forfeiting millions of dollars and making huge drug interdictions with the Florida Joint Task Force Group; and that he knew once I graduated, I'd leave. He was right!"

"So, he punished you by transferring you out of OCB and sticking you on midnights in District 1...on the desk?" Vince said, smirking knowingly.

"Nope," Rick said with a grin. "I beat him to the punch. I knew he'd try to bury me down south, so I had already set things in motion. I met with Station 1's major—great guy; he desperately needed a Spanish-speaking Uniform officer on mids. Thank God that type of transfer doesn't need the director's approval."

"Genius, Rick. But how will you manage 10:00 p.m. to 6:00 a.m.?"

"I picked Friday to Saturday off so I can catch up on sleep." Rick held up a finger. "I get off my shift, crash from 6:30 to 8:00 in the morning."

Another finger. "Classes run to 9:00 a.m. to 5:00 p.m., so I'm home by 5:30."

Third and last finger. "I will rest up on my days off." He exhaled, almost laughing at the absurdity. "I'm asleep by 6:00 p.m., up 9:00 p.m., and I whip up a quick dinner." He shrugged. "Then I roll into the station, and I try to nap in my car during lunch."

"That's *insane*," Vince said.

"Yup, that's what the dean told me last week."

Vince huffed a small laugh. "Well, Rick...if anyone can pull that off, it's you. See you in class."

They fell into step for a moment, the line moving forward inch by inch, until Vince peeled off toward his building.

• • •

The weeks passed in a steady, relentless rhythm—long classes, minimal sleep, and the constant shuffle between lectures and parking lot power naps. Law school was manageable for Rick, except when it came to his Contracts course and the exhaustion that seemed to shadow every hour. He actually mastered sleeping upright with his head in his hands, elbows planted firmly on the desk, a skill that quickly became essential to his survival.

For lunch, he'd escape to the parking lot, start the car, blast the AC into freezing sleep mode, and drift into a half-conscious nap. Vince would go grab lunch, returning ten minutes before the next afternoon class with a cheeseburger and a small Coke.

The knock on the driver's window startled Rick every single time, pulling him just enough from his daze. Visine in hand, he squeezed a few burning drops into his eyes, wincing as the sting chased away the fog of sleep. He tore into half the BK cheeseburger, washed it down with slow sips of Coke, and felt the caffeine-like fuel, though it barely kicked in. He crumpled the wrapper, vaulted out of the car, and raced across the lot toward his 1:00 p.m. class.

Halfway through the semester, practice midterms loomed, and Rick was struggling to retain even the most fundamental principles of Contracts, in particular—a royal nightmare.

"Mr. Diaz, please explain the holding of *Hadley v. Baxendale,*" Professor Kennedy asked.

"Uh...well, it had to do with damages?" Rick ventured.

"Yes, go on."

"Uh...the damages you can recover?"

"And?"

"And they have to be reasonable."

"Good, but there's more—the most important part."

Rick had read the case, but it was Friday, and sleep deprivation had taxed his brain cells. An uncomfortable silence settled over the classroom.

"Mr. Diaz, I expect you to be better prepared the next time I call on you. *Hadley* is the cornerstone of any breach of contract claim. It's all—and only—about damages. And it's not that hard."

Concepts like anticipatory breach, the rule against perpetuities, unilateral mistake of fact, and rescission loomed over Rick. And then there was the dreaded UCC, the Uniform Commercial Code. A contract concept of business dealings—a virtual nightmare disguised as a helpful guide. It was supposed to make disputed business transactions across states consistent. But to Rick, it might as well have been written in hieroglyphics.

Professor Kennedy was the tougher of the two Contracts professors in the building. Rick caught himself wishing he'd landed in Section B instead...but then he wouldn't see Vinny as much. And somehow, that made the punishment feel a little more bearable.

Contracts was a two-semester class. At Christmas break, Rick got an A in Criminal Law and Criminal Procedure, three C's, and the much-anticipated D—in Contracts.

Fuck. He'd need at least a B in Contracts next semester, or he was done.

After the first year, nearly a quarter of Section A—fifteen to twenty students—had dropped out. The pressure had been brutal, the grind relentless. Rick survived.

When the second-semester Contracts classes resumed, Professor Kennedy wasted no time calling on Rick and, once again, he belittled him in front of everyone. Same condescending tone. Same smug look.

At lunch, Rick went to his office and asked for a meeting. Kennedy didn't seem surprised—he was almost amused.

"You know," the professor said, leaning back in his chair, "you were the only D last semester. Unless you pull off a B this term, you can't continue here."

Rick took a deep breath. "Sir, what I'm about to say *might* get me kicked out of this school."

Kennedy raised an eyebrow. "I'm listening."

"I know I'm struggling. It's not from a lack of preparation; I just don't get many of the concepts. But you know what separates us? I'm a cop. I help people. I save people. I've been yelled at, kicked, punched, shot at, and I always show up. I make decisions that change lives. I decide whether someone gets cuffs or a second chance. That's real power. And I don't abuse it."

Rick let out a frustrated breath. "You do. Why? You humiliate students who aren't as sharp as your favorites—Dave and Eileen—simply because you can. But understand something. Even though you'd probably love to watch me fail out of law school...if you collapse in class tomorrow, I'd be the first one to jump and do CPR to try and save your life. I am assigned to this *fucking* district, and when on patrol, I drive through *this* campus."

Rick pushed back his chair and stood. His voice stayed even. "If you're not willing to help me, just say so. I'll withdraw here and now. But I'm not giving you the satisfaction of dragging me in front of classmates, none of whom ever had to fucking work a damn day in their lives—let alone done what I do."

Kennedy stared at him for a moment, his face giving nothing away. Rick kept his fear buried deep, locked behind a steady stare.

At last, Kennedy spoke—quietly, almost level. "I didn't know you were working as a police officer *and* attending school.

He gazed outside the window, stood up, and walked toward it. Seconds seemed like minutes.

Here it comes, Rick thought.

"You're going to need a speed course on semester one. Without mastering what you missed there, you won't survive semester two. You need to command the basics of Contracts. Forget the Socratic method—we'll do this a different way. What's your last class on Fridays?"

"Three," Rick answered.

"Very well. We'll start this Friday. Plan to stay after five if necessary." No more needed to be said.

Rick showed up for every tutorial. Kennedy dropped the theatrics—the cold calls, the case debates. Instead, he stripped Contracts down to its bones—Contracts 101—simple, methodical, and direct, the way Rick learned best.

After three sessions, it all clicked. Offer, acceptance, consideration—suddenly it all made sense. When finals came, Rick nailed the exam with a B+.

A week later, Kennedy caught him in the hallway. "Mr. Diaz," he said, almost in passing, "your exam...it was a solid B, but I bumped it to a B+."

Rick frowned slightly. "Why?"

"I spoke with Vince Farina. I never knew you two worked together...or that he trained you." Kennedy straightened his tie, his voice softening. "He told me a lot about you. That plus is more than well-earned—it's deserved."

Rick didn't say a word. He just nodded, understanding that—for once—he and Kennedy saw each other eye-to-eye.

• • •

By the second year, Rick had carved a rhythm that was near perfect: lectures, midnight shifts at Station 1, stolen moments of sleep, and even squeezed in a part-time job at a local debt collection law firm.

Wednesday and Friday afternoons offered rare pockets of freedom at the law firm—Rick turned them into work hours, dialing debtors, drafting lawsuits, and preparing discovery. Even the mundane was executed with exacting efficiency, as though his life depended on it. He was now getting hands-on experience working with lawyers in a real law-practicing setting.

Then came the winter break of Rick's second year, and life demanded a rare detour: He got married. Rick made what he would later call the greatest decision of his life.

It was a Friday night, and the ceremony drew 400 guests, grand yet intimate in its own way. The vows carried quiet gravity, a recognition that this was the one anchor he would not let slip. His wife knew the weight of his world without needing to ask.

By midday Saturday, the newlyweds were airborne to Cancun, escaping chaos for a short two-day honeymoon weekend. They returned Monday, missing only a single class that day. Rick moved through it all with the same exacting discipline he applied to every part of his life. Even his marriage was treated with measured care, every moment accounted for, every hour respected.

Rick's wife's family owned a well-known auto dealership, a business with a general counsel—Daniel Montero—who was loud, flamboyant, and impossible to ignore.

By the end of the second year, the class had now thinned to roughly fifty students.

Law school year three for Rick was more of a formality than a challenge. The color of the tassel, his mid-range rank in Section A—none of it mattered. By now, he had proven himself as a law student, and the school had finally earned its accreditation.

Classes were now predictable, a refining year for most students, a way to stretch out tuition and maintain appearances that a law degree required endless struggle. Rick moved through it with focus, steady and unshaken, already preparing for what came next: the bar exam.

Rick took a six-week leave of absence. No watch, no clock. No dinners. No parties. No movies. No fishing. No nothing. He ate when hungry, slept when tired. Every other moment, he studied.

He was ready.

IX
THE OATH

Rick was fortunate as OIC (Officer in Charge) Platoon Commander on the Miami Lakes station midnight shift—no injuries to Platoon officers meant he could stay in the station for most shifts, working at the front desk. No patrols, no dispatch calls to answer, just administrative work, answering phones, and studying. He handled the daily paperwork like a lightning rod, clearing the desk by midnight and giving himself six straight hours to focus on his law books. That quiet time was his lifeline.

Mids were ghostly hours. From midnight to 5:00 a.m., Rick was often the only soul inside the quiet station. Occasionally, an injured officer on light duty meant Rick had to hit the road and patrol in a marked unit. He didn't mind. An occasional change in pace was refreshing and kept Rick sharp. Quiet, empty streets, minimal distraction, time to think. The midnight had a slow rhythm, a way of speaking if you listened. The tempo seemed to be slower, though it was not. Reflection wasn't easy from 6:00 a.m. to midnight. On these shifts, Rick's time was his alone.

For the first time in his life, Rick broke a lifelong habit—

he drank coffee. Fucking Kojak had been prophetic. Now, five years later, Rick finally understood why. It was better than the Vivarin, over-the-counter caffeine tablets Rick took once and then immediately felt the onset of a heart attack.

Generally, midnight shifts were mercifully uncomplicated. Even criminals need to sleep. Rick's shift included one extreme alcoholic lieutenant, a few rookie sergeants, and maybe a total of ten officers. They were all easy—the rookies were marginally functional.

Rick made all of their jobs simpler for the officers and sergeants; he reviewed their reports, corrected every grammar slip, and caught every typo. Not a single officer or civilian complaint landed on the sergeant or lieutenant's desk.

They all knew why Rick was so helpful. He was preparing to leave the department, maximizing the tuition reimbursement program: 50 percent back, but only with a B or better—a tall order for a first-year law student, but he was determined. The midnight sergeants, and the drunken lieutenant who was quietly aware, covered for him.

On especially slow nights, officers would relieve him for a sneak sleeping break in the gym and locker rooms, which offered the perfect escape hideaway. Huge, empty, silent, dark. Rick had stashed a pillow and blanket among his gear in his locker.

Once the lights went out, he could sometimes stretch his twelve longer than the thirty minutes allotted. As long as his relief buddy wasn't dispatched, he got the rare luxury of uninterrupted rest for maybe a full hour.

Whenever a marked unit pulled into the station, the officer covering Rick's desk duty would glance at the markings. If it were a supervisor, they would rush into the locker room and wake Rick up. In an instant, Rick would snap to, shove his pillow and blanket back into the locker, saddle on his gear, and dash to the front desk. His relief buddy would go back on patrol, and it would look like business as usual.

One morning, as Rick was clocking out after a quiet night on patrol, his sergeant stopped him at the door. "Diaz, step into my office for a second."

Rick followed him in.

The sergeant closed the door and handed him his worksheet. "Rick, look at your worksheet."

Rick scanned it. "And?"

"Look at your total patrol miles for your unit's odometer for the eight-hour shift on your worksheet. *Three* miles?"

Rick's eyes dropped to the numbers. "*Shit*," he muttered. "Yeah...I see it."

The daily worksheet was every cop's paper trail for their shift—dispatch times, arrivals, every call handled, reports, tickets written, and less importantly, the mileage during the hours of patrol. Each shift began and ended with odometer readings on the daily activity log. The subtraction math was easy. A typical patrol shift should put anywhere from seventy-five to 125 miles on the cruiser.

"I know what you're doing, and I don't give a damn, Rick," the sergeant said, leaning back in his chair. "None of us do. Not even the lieutenant. But upstairs? They notice that shit. You need to figure it out. Doesn't matter when you're on the desk, but I can't show you as a ghost when you're on the road."

Rick nodded. "Yes, Sarge. I know. Thanks."

The sergeant just grunted. "Get some rest."

Three miles. "*Three lousy miles*," Rick muttered to himself. "Damn, I should have known better." He needed to find a way to fix this. And he would...

The next time Rick had to patrol the district, he stuck to his usual routine, but with one clever twist. From 10:00 p.m.

to midnight, he "jumped" all calls he could, grabbing them immediately, even when they weren't assigned to him. It wasn't about showing off; it was a calculated strategy. After midnight, his squadmates handled the bulk of calls, giving Rick uninterrupted hours to study.

Midnights could be boring—but they could turn deadly in an instant, like that morning at the North Miami Beach bank five years earlier.

Midnight struck and became the witching hour. Having covered so many calls for his buddies, Rick then set up his unit backed in by a wall in a U-shaped industrial park—safe from rear ambushes, with a clear line of sight in every direction. He would flip through his law books with his car parked, lower the radio, and respond only to any "3-call"—high-priority situations. He was almost always the first one on the scene, and everyone on the midnight platoon noticed. Rick was "forgiven" for his absence on nonemergency calls.

By now, every squad on midnight patrol knew and respected him. With only five years on the job, a tour in OCB and the title OIC, surviving the day four shoot-out, and a year of law school under his belt, he'd earned a reputation that kept him untouchable. Nobody was going to rat him out.

Rick came up with a fix for the odometer miles problem. On his road patrol nights, starting at 5:00 a.m., he'd pack up his law books and then—which did not happen often—do high-speed laps on the Palmetto Expressway, State Road 826, in Miami Lakes. He went seventy-five miles per hour for forty-five minutes, weaving up and down the highway, then exiting and circling back the opposite way like an oval racetrack.

Then, at about 5:45 a.m., he'd pull into the station, unload the unit, turn in his reports, and 06 [cancel out the shift] on the radio. In that time, he'd log about forty-five miles on the odometer—just enough to not arouse any suspicion that he might be sleeping on duty and not handling calls. It worked for the next three years.

One night, an anonymous call reported that a marked unit was speeding without lights or sirens on the Palmetto. The lieutenant ordered a roll call over the radio and asked for the location of every officer. He had no choice. Everyone knew it was Rick—even the drunk lieutenant.

Rick calmly exited the nearest off-ramp and went like a beeline for the station. When the dispatcher asked for his location, Rick replied only, "I'm arriving 05 [at the station]," leaving out how far from the station he actually was.

When the dispatcher reported that no officer admitted being on the Palmetto, the lieutenant asked, "Was that an anonymous caller?"

"QSL," the dispatcher replied.

"QSL," the lieutenant muttered—an unspoken. He *knew* who it was. But with an anonymous caller, thankfully and luckily, it ended there. No need to investigate further or generate a report.

Still curious, at the end of the shift, the lieutenant pulled Rick aside. "It was you, wasn't it?"

"Lieutenant...that sounds like a rhetorical question," Rick replied with a smile. "Aren't you gonna read me my rights?"

"Fuck you, Diaz, you're not a lawyer yet. Just be careful. Whenever you come upon a civilian vehicle during your racetrack circuit on the highway slow it down."

Rick smiled but gave no admission or false denial. Silence was the easy way to do the tightrope walk.

Around 1:00 a.m., Rick was heading to the department's Communications Bureau—twenty miles from Station 1—to hand-deliver the Daily Commander's Report and the driver-violation-ticket transmittal batch. The expressway was deserted, and fog had settled in. Rick was doing about sixty miles per hour.

Suddenly, a bright flash appeared in Rick's rearview mirror. A car—wide, fast—was closing in on his marked Ford Crown Victoria. He estimated its speed at 100 miles per hour. Unknown occupants. Police cars *weren't* bulletproof. Rick had six rounds in his revolver, plus the two issued speedloaders with twelve more rounds. He had put a lot of drug traffickers away for long prison terms—one even threatened he'd kill Rick once he got released from prison.

Paranoid? Maybe. But there wasn't much time to react. If he called a 315 for assistance and it was just a speeding motorist, it could be seen as him overreacting. But if it was a hit, and Rick didn't call for backup, it could be far worse.

Rick gripped the mic, pressed it to his mouth, and keyed in his unit number. "Ten-fifty?" His voice carried urgency—fast, clipped.

The dispatcher answered immediately, "Ten-fifty, QSK."

Rick slowed, moving to the right lane as he began to exit, drawing the potential threat closer, making himself an easier target but still tactically safe. The BMW stayed in the left-most lane and continued racing south. Relief washed over him. This wasn't what he feared.

"Ten-fifty, QRU?"

Rick's hand hovered over the mic. He keyed the mic.

"Ten-fifty, QSL. Disregard for now."

The channel fell quiet. Every officer listening knew something was up. Curiosity buzzed across the squad. Rick was known for not initiating anything on mids. In a way, he had become like Vince before he was cleared. Any enforcement action meant writing a bunch of reports and maybe having to go to court. Rick could not afford to miss a law class for a ticket hearing.

He jumped back up and onto the highway at the next entrance. He floored the Crown Vic, the tires screaming against the asphalt. The needle climbed—100, 110, 120, 127 miles per hour. The BMW ahead held its line in the left lane.

Rick hit the lights, siren, and spotlight full-on. The white BMW's brakes locked, tires smoking, the car skidding toward the shoulder. A cloud of white smoke surrounded the vehicle. It was the sign of panic, not a threat.

One occupant. Black male. Rick's seat belt snagged for a second, then gave way. He stepped out, gun drawn, every nerve on fire. The driver's door swung open. The man stepped out fast—too fast—and thrust his right hand forward. Something black in his right hand caught the direct lights.

Rick froze for half a breath. *What the hell was that?* His instincts screamed *gun*. What else could it be? Who would be so damn stupid to *point anything else at a cop* in the dark? Every training, every simulation, every call he'd ever run all came rushing back. But this time, Rick had the edge. He had target acquisition, the faster draw.

The subject was facing Rick's cruiser head-on, the glare of the spotlight washing over him. Rick's heart was thundering.

Damn it, he thought, *I should've called for backup. Too late now.*

The driver's right hand still clutched that dark object, rising higher.

Rick's finger tightened on the trigger, milliseconds from breaking the first shot—when suddenly, the man's hand shot straight up, the black object glinting in the air.

"Don't shoot! Don't shoot! Don't shoot!"

The driver stood frozen, rigid as ice. Rick could not rule out the object as a gun. This was one of those nights where every wrong guess could cost him his life.

He shoved the barrel forward and barked, "Don't you fucking move! Drop it! Slowly! *Now!*"

The man immediately obeyed, hands shaking.

"Turn around. Face away from me. Slowly—real slowly—take out your driver's license with your right hand but keep your left arm up."

The space Rick set brought control to the encounter. Rick keyed the mic, now took a 19, and asked for backup—routine on paper, but every cop listening on that frequency knew better.

Units rolled out fast, like it was a 315—Rick pulling someone over: It had to be more than a bullshit traffic violation.

While the driver slowly reached for his license, Rick kept talking, deliberate, steady. He wanted the man's mind occupied, pulled into dialogue rather than drifting toward confrontation.

"Okay, walk back five steps, still facing away from me. Don't turn around. Take one step at a time. Now put the license on the trunk with your right hand.

"Now, take ten steps forward—don't turn around, don't move your hands. Keep them both above your head."

Rick's commands were as clear as they were stern.

"All right," he said, steady but sharp, "what's your name?"

"Mark Duper."

Rick blinked. "The Dolphins' wide receiver? Get the fuck out of here. You're not Mark Duper."

"I am, officer."

Rick grabbed the Florida driver's license from the top of

the trunk. It was official-looking. The name read *Mark Super Duper*. Rick frowned. The guy was maybe five-nine.

"Sir, that's a fake name, and you're too short to be an NFL wide receiver."

"Officer, my phone is on the floor. I was talking to my agent. He's probably still on the line—he'll tell you it's me. Please, check it."

Rick leaned down, grabbed the phone, and sure enough—the call was still connected. The voice on the other end confirmed everything: The driver was coming back from a house party in Weston. Tiffany watches for the offensive line—it was in the brand's featured turquoise box sitting on the front seat.

Rick keyed the radio again. "Ten-fifty—cancel backup. Signal 19 resolved."

Later, when the other responding units found out, they were half relieved, half pissed—they'd wanted autographs. The Miami Dolphins were having a hot season that year, and for a second, Rick had almost ended one of their best players' careers.

Sitting alone in his cruiser afterward, Rick stared at his hands. The adrenaline rush was receding, replaced by the slow ache and reflection that came after a close call.

Rick got back into the patrol car, turned the key, merged back onto the dark highway, and drove into the quiet. Another night survived. The encounter only confirmed that this career change had been the right decision. Graduation from law school was close now.

Next time, should he have let the speeder keep going, and if the man killed himself, so be it? The other part of Rick would never allow someone that reckless to take an innocent person with him.

On graduation day, rather than the dean giving it to him,

Professor Kennedy handed Rick his diploma. "Congrats, very well done." Nothing more needed to be said.

It was now time for Rick to register for the Florida Bar Exam—the test that would finally give him the authority to practice law. Every late night, every skipped meal, every moment of stolen sleep had led to this. The final stretch. St. Thomas had just received its accreditation six months earlier.

To study for the exam, Rick burned a lot of his PTO. For two months, it was all study, all focus. No parties, no concerts, no beach, no distractions. He hid his watch and took the clock off the wall. Slept when tired, ate when hungry, studied when awake. BLE 49—a survivor. No parties, no movies, no beach, no life. Just outlines, case law, and caffeine.

When test day came, Rick treated it like a high-risk call: precise, methodical, every second critical. He left the testing center earlier than all of the others. Some looked at him in astonishment. Rick was drained but confident, knowing he had pushed himself to the absolute limit.

On a policeman's salary, there wasn't money for much fanfare—just a warm family gathering and a simple congratulatory dinner. Rick had made it.

Months later, Rick received his results—passed. The next day, he was sworn in as a Florida lawyer. The federal bar followed the next week, and he passed that one, too. Daniel Montero wasted no time hiring Rick full-time, but Rick still wanted a gold badge.

He made an appointment with the police department director.

Rick was blunt. "I have nine years here—an impeccable record and now, a law degree. Years ago, you denied my LOA, because you said I'd leave once I became a lawyer. Well, I'm here now. Appoint me commander and assign me wherever you want—communications, investigations, patrol, or the legal unit. I'll stay for at least one more year."

"Denied," said the director.

"Understood." Rick reached into his briefcase and tendered his resignation.

Rick went back to the station for one last time. He emptied his locker, threw out the pillow and blanket. "I won't need these guys anymore," he said aloud.

He said goodbye to his MDPD Station 1 buddies, each handshake heavy with history and a different story.

He leaned down toward the drunk lieutenant and asked for permission to give a final EOW—end of watch.

The lieutenant's head bobbed in a slow, heavy nod. "Had you not asked, I would have ordered it," he said.

Rick walked up to the front desk, grabbed the mic, and took a moment. Looking all around at his surroundings, he keyed the radio, thumb hovering for a beat he couldn't quite hide.

"Ten-fifty?"

A calm voice answered almost instantly—Jesse—the veteran, and the best dispatcher MDPD ever had.

"Ten-fifty, QSK?"

He stood there surrounded by his buddies—every one of them quiet, watching. No jokes, no sarcasm, just a circle of men and women waiting for a moment they all looked forward to. They were both happy and sad, but also understood.

Rick swallowed hard. His hand tightened around the mic.

"Ten-fifty is 06...for the last time." Rick took a breath before continuing. "Show me EOW."

A pause followed. It was brief, but those words were crushing. Then, Jesse's voice returned, softer than anyone had ever heard her on the air: "Ten-fifty… All of us bid you good luck and farewell."

The words landed heavier than he expected—final, irreversible, and loud in the silence that followed. His buddies didn't cheer. They didn't move. They just stood there, letting the weight of it settle, knowing they were witnessing the exact second Rick's life shifted into something new. One last duty: to return his departmental equipment.

At the quartermaster's office, he turned in all of his gear as required. "Keep your badge," the sergeant told him. "Technically, you don't have ten years on, and it's not an official retirement—but you've earned the right to keep it."

Then he drove away from the station he had called home for years, never looking back. The streets, the midnight patrols, the danger—they were all behind him now.

Rick held the badge in his hand for a long moment. A single tear slid down his cheek. He remembered the way his mother pinned it on his uniform for the first time, nine years earlier. His first call after departing the quartermaster's office was to her, and the next was to his wife.

Rick felt the weight of what he had accomplished. His call sign, Defender, would stay with him forever. It was no longer about protecting people in the streets or standing between danger and the innocent. Now, it meant defending people in a courtroom—another type of battlefield.

X
THE CHASE

"Let's get on the same page. You know these guys aren't surrendering," Lindner said, eyes locked on the road ahead. His voice was flat, accepting the inevitable. "We're gonna have to take them out."

"Yep," Mateo replied, "they are calm, *way too calm*."

"Who the fuck do they think they are?"

"Criminals," Mateo said flatly. "They had the balls to do a daytime armed robbery in Coral Gables and shoot a lady in the head? Every jewelry store has a buzzer system nowadays, so they had to look like customers first. Once they were in, it was game on. Then, they dump the getaway vehicle, hijack a UPS truck, *and* take its driver hostage? They planned it out carefully."

Lindner shook his head. "How the fuck Gables PD didn't find 'em in the city before they escaped beats me."

"They're always braggin' about having the fastest response time in the country," Mateo said, glancing at the dashboard.

"How's the gas looking?" Lindner asked.

Mateo kept his eyes on the road. "We're burning a lot fast."

Lindner leaned back, exhaling hard. "You think the mall rep's gonna be pissed we left the detail?"

Mateo chuckled. "Stop worrying about that dude. Probably. Today might've been our last day working there. I'll check with the sergeant tomorrow, see if we're still on the schedule. If not, there's a bunch of off-duty gigs this time of year. I hear Dadeland and Dolphin Malls are short."

"Yeah, the food's good there, too," Lindner said.

Mateo grinned. "True. But the chicks at Dolphin Mall? Prettier. Hotter."

"You're not lyin'. The Venezuelans and Colombians? Jesus. They're way different."

"Yeah, but it's all plastic surgery, dude," Mateo said. "Costs half down there. Don't forget the Brazilians."

"I don't speak Portuguese," Lindner replied.

"It's *bela,*" Mateo said.

"Bella?"

"No, dumbass—*B-E-L-A*. That's all you need to start a conversation."

"Really? B-E-L-A?"

"Yep."

"You speak Portuguese?"

"A bit."

"Okay, then how do you say, 'Can I get your number?'"

Mateo laughed. "Hell if I know."

They both laughed—the kind of laugh that was half nerves, half habit. They were still a bit behind. But they were almost flying. Now, they estimated ten minutes to intersect the truck.

Then Lindner's radio crackled. "Hold up...update coming through."

"What's up?"

"Fucking media chopper still on them; air unit is still catching up. They are giving live reports over television."

"Come on," Mateo said. "You don't know that."

"Yeah, I do. Listen." He turned the volume up. "They're live. Breaking news."

"You know what that means?" Mateo said.

"Yeah—a bird's-eye view."

Mateo shook his head. "Nah, man. It gives everyone a bird's-eye view. Wouldn't it be something if we could stream it here?"

Lindner reached for his laptop. "Hold up...maybe I can pull it up." He waited, then shut the computer. "Fuck, I can't stream it. We are moving too much."

"I don't know if we can catch up in time—we're getting real low."

"Keep going, bro. If we run out, we run out. That truck's gotta be low, too."

Lindner nodded, eyes still locked ahead. "Just punch it. Don't lose your brakes—they're probably white-hot by now."

"I know," Mateo said. "I can smell it."

The cruiser rattled and shook as the speed climbed, needle edging into the red. Sirens howled over the highway, red-and-blue lights painting the median in violent rhythm. Mateo's grip on the wheel was tight, the radio chatter bleeding through the static.

"They ain't getting away," he said, eyes locked on the taillights of the UPS truck ahead. "We got ground, we got air. We got enough units."

Lindner snorted. "No, dude—we got *too many* units, and a lot of PRT are now close behind the truck, so we're good to go."

He shifted in his seat, glancing at the speedometer as the needle trembled near the red. The truck barreled forward, weaving through traffic like a tank with nothing left to lose.

"Where the fuck is FHP?" Mateo asked. "They're the ones allowed to PIT maneuver."

"Who knows?." Lindner said. "They're not on our frequency either. Maybe they are setting up somewhere. But with a hostage inside, and now that it's getting to rush hour traffic in the city, that's a risk. I heard on the radio that the hostage was in the middle of the two subjects—probably not even strapped in."

Mateo's jaw grinded. "That's right. Probably why they won't PIT. Too dangerous." He paused, then snapped, "Is it any riskier than what they're doing right now? Hell no. They can ram cars on 75, kill the hostage, shoot at civilians—it's *all* dangerous."

"You're right," Lindner said, squinting through the flashing chaos ahead. "Remember, sounds like both are armed. They might have extra clips."

Mateo didn't respond. The wail of the sirens and the thrum of the engine filled the silence until Lindner cursed under his breath. "Fuck the math on their ammo. Watch that car coming up on your right! Jesus Christ, don't they hear the siren? See the lights? No brake lights either. What a dickhead!"

"Maybe he don't know that. Even stupid people deserve the benefit of any doubt," Mateo muttered.

Lindner shot him a look. "Now you sound like a defense attorney, man."

"Yeah," Mateo said with a bitter laugh. "Fucking defense attorneys. Make all that money off technicalities and bullshit just to win a case. Fucking lawyers—all the same. Money, money, money."

Lindner barked a short laugh. "Shit, you pay for one!"

Mateo glanced over, brow furrowed. "Man, what are you talking about?"

"The PBA," Lindner said.

"Nah, that's the union."

"Yeah, genius, but you don't know that part of your

PBA dues goes for lawyers in case they need to appoint one to you?"

Mateo opened his mouth, but the radio cracked alive before he could respond. Sirens pulsed in the background, and Lindner's eyes narrowed at the GPS.

"Hold on, man. Sounds like them boys are getting off I-75. This shit's gonna get tight." He tapped the dashboard. "We're catching up, but under an eighth of a tank. Fuck—imagine running out of gas. Did you top off this morning?"

Mateo grinned. "My gun or my gas?"

"Both, dude."

"My gun—always. Not the gas tank. I had just under three-quarters, figured for the off-duty, I was good. I should have; the pumps were only a few minutes away."

Lindner shook his head. "Hope you learned a lesson. Top off the tank every morning, no matter what. Look at us now—imagine running out before we take these fucks down. They'll laugh their asses off at us."

Mateo's eyes darted between lanes. "You know, we could stop at a gas station, take on a quarter in two minutes, haul ass, and make up the time."

Lindner turned to him, incredulously. "Are you out of your fucking mind? Can you imagine how that'll look? Folks there will call 911 first thing—say we're out of jurisdiction, and that we pulled in on emergency mode just to gas up."

Mateo lifted a hand in surrender. "Okay, okay. Bad idea. Jeez." Both of his hands fell back on the steering wheel.

"No! It's a *very* bad idea," Lindner snapped. "And if that's the reason we don't get there in time, we're the dicks."

Mateo exhaled through his nose. "Yep, Monday-morning quarterbacks. You just know it's coming: *Why so many units? Why no PIT? Why didn't you just let them drive until they ran out of gas?*"

"Oh, yeah," Lindner said, nodding. "And if they kill a few civilians because of that, the media will flip it around and criticize us anyway."

Mateo gave a dry laugh. "And then the lawyers will sue us no matter what."

Mateo stared straight ahead. For a few seconds, nothing but the wind and the sound of the engine filled the cabin. The UPS truck loomed larger in the distance. Every mile felt like a lifetime, every second a coin toss between justice and catastrophe. The sirens wailed, distant helicopters circling above chaos.

"Well, we've got our mission," he said quietly. "Remember Scot Anderson? I ain't doing that."

Lindner glanced over, meeting his eyes for a beat. "You mean *we* ain't doing that."

Mateo smirked, steadying the wheel as the highway bent ahead. "Fucking A."

"Speaking of…" said Lindner, then shook his head. "I'd forgotten our PBA dues include free legal representation."

Mateo smirked. "Do you get to pick your own lawyer?"

"I don't know, I doubt it," Lindner said, tightening his grip on the grab handle above the unit's passenger door.

"I'd pick Troy White," Mateo said. "Badass motherfucker."

"The best," Lindner agreed. "He got those City of Miami cops off—can't remember their names."

"Alvaro and Manzano," Mateo answered instantly.

Lindner glanced over, half in disbelief. "Remind me to pick you next time we play Trivial Pursuit. How the hell do you know all this? That was, what, thirty, forty years ago?"

"I'm reading his book," Mateo said. "*White's Law.*"

"Of course you are."

"Dude got big-time cocaine traffickers off, that famous race car driver, and a bunch of celebrities."

"So?" Lindner asked, watching the highway narrow ahead. He whistled low. "Yeah, the PBA ain't giving us Troy White if we ever need a lawyer."

Mateo chuckled. "Maybe not. But I know of a guy like that. He's tight with the PBA. Used to be a cop."

"A retired lawyer?"

"No," Mateo said, shaking his head. "Retired cop. Still a lawyer."

"You know him, or you just know of him?"

Mateo smiled. "I don't, but he's former MDPD. Big cases, big balls. Represented dopers in Colombia—the real bosses. Speaking of big-time drug traffickers, guess what?"

"What?"

"He represented Willy Falcon."

"You're shitting me."

"Not a bit. This guy got Willy a deal for twenty. Sal Magluta got supermax for 200 years, but Willy? Out. Lawyer even got him to avoid deportation to Cuba—so long as he left the US."

Lindner laughed. "So, he did a Free Willy?"

"You're an asshole," Mateo said, laughing despite himself. "But yeah. Badass lawyer."

"Ain't no way the PBA's got someone like that on their list," Lindner said.

"Hell no. But get this—Oscar knows him. Real well."

"Ordiales?" Lindner said, surprised.

"Yep. His name is Rick something."

"You're shittin' me."

"Nope. Small world."

Lindner shook his head, a crooked grin cutting through the tension. "That's good to know."

"Yeah," Mateo said, eyes still on the flashing truck ahead. "It's good to know…'cause you never know."

5:28 p.m.

The radio hissed again, a voice breaking through the static. The chase was tightening. The colloquy and laughter died. They were now three minutes to getting within a good enough distance to matter.

XI
VALENTINE'S DAY

By 2018, Rick was three decades into criminal defense practice, experienced enough to recognize patterns rather than exceptions. That changed on February 14, 2018.

What should have been a day of lighthearted distraction at Marjory Stoneman Douglas High School in Parkland, Florida became one of the darkest in modern American memory. That afternoon, Nathaniel Cross, a nineteen-year-old former student, entered the campus carrying an AR-15 rifle and a backpack filled with ammunition and a lot of it. He went there with minimal skill but with great preparation and callousness.

The kid knew the layout of the school all too well. He had walked through those halls many times before as a student, but now, on this day, he was an angry predator, hungry for a mass casualty and hunting down his prey. Moving through the empty corridors, looking for easy targets, he found a fertile zone and opened fire in classrooms, hallways, at anyone he could catch in his path.

While the gunfire erupted, multiple calls poured into 911—the Broward County Sheriff's Office [BSO].

"Attention, all units, shots fired at Marjory Stoneman Douglas High School, 5901 Pine Island Road, Parkland—active shooter—no other information at this time," the dispatcher said.

The shooting seemed to last forever. When the last round was fired, seventeen people were dead—fourteen students, three staff—and seventeen more were wounded. The scale and horror of the violence stunned the nation; it was over before most students, teachers, and other faculty members even had a chance to realize what was happening.

Broward County's extensive school police network was meant to keep students safe. It had school resource officers stationed at every public institution. The first officer to respond, Deputy Scot Anderson, was assigned to and posted at that campus. Yet, when those shots rang out, Anderson did not move toward the crackling of gunfire; he did not enter the building. Instead, he took cover outside, remaining there for several critical minutes as the massacre continued inside.

While terrified and panicked students hid beneath desks and whispered to 911 operators, Anderson stayed positioned behind a structured column. His inaction became a national flashpoint—raising questions about duty, courage, and accountability in a school security system already under scrutiny. Some legal analysts insisted his conduct fell within "common" response patterns under stress. But anyone with military or law-enforcement blood saw it for what it was: unacceptable. They despised him for it.

Whether out of ammunition, remaining live students, or both, Cross escaped the classroom, leaving a bloody trail of his shooting victims behind. He walked through the halls like a ghost, slipping away, disappearing from and beyond the school grounds as the sirens of dozens of police patrol cars rushing to the school wailed in the distance. Multiple perimeters were set up. He appeared to have escaped, but a few hours later, amid the hum of the otherwise ordinary day, he was found by the police sitting in the dining room at a nearby McDonald's. He was calm and collected, almost oblivious to the world he had just shattered, not far behind the restaurant.

That day not only changed the lives of some three dozen families, but also exposed deep fractures in law enforcement's response, school safety procedures, and the moral expectation placed on those sworn to protect our children, especially while in school.

The shooting received continued nationwide attention similar to the Sandy Hook and Columbine school shootings. Cross was tried as an adult. He pled guilty to all counts, having a trial only to challenge the penalty of the death sentence. He got thirty-four life sentences. Efforts to impose the death penalty failed when the trial jury—after hearing aggravating and mitigating evidence—voted nine to three for the death penalty—insufficient to meet the unanimity requirement.

Shortly after that sentence, the Florida legislature modified that law to allow the sentencing judge to impose the death penalty with a nonunanimous jury recommendation of eight out of twelve jurors. Despite killing over a dozen students and school staff, Nathaniel Cross's life was spared.

Anderson quickly earned the grim nickname "The Coward from Broward." Indicted on seventeen counts of child neglect and an equal number of counts of culpable negligence, his case drew nationwide attention and debate over his inaction. It was a media frenzy. The gravamen of the charges centered on one damning allegation: his failure to act. His refusal to locate, identify, and eliminate the threat—the active shooter, Cross, to survive himself. It stood in stark contrast to the oath every Florida officer took: a promise to perform their duties faithfully and without hesitation, "so help me God."

Anderson was represented by a highly skilled middle-aged criminal defense attorney from Miami. The lawyer immediately pursued Florida's controversial stand-your-ground defense, filing motions to have all charges dismissed. The court denied those motions following a nonjury minitrial, and the full trial commenced on May 21, 2023.

Four days later, after deliberations, the jury delivered a verdict: Anderson was acquitted of all charges. Most observers were stunned, but this was, after all, a Broward County jury—those who knew what that meant weren't much surprised.

The backbone of the defense hinged on a precise, technical argument: The gunshots appeared to originate outside the building where the shooting occurred. To substantiate this, twenty witnesses were called. Among them, another Parkland resource officer testified on Anderson's behalf, trying to underscore the chaos and perceived threat the officer faced.

The prosecution struggled to mount a convincing rebuttal. All that was needed was one pointed question—the kind that might leave a defendant without a clear answer, both procedurally and practically: *Why didn't he move toward the source of the shots, or at least where he believed they were coming from, as required by his oath?*

By the trial's end, the acquittal left the public polarized—some outraged, others quietly nodding to the legal arguments—but all captivated by the drama of a trial that had become a national spectacle. Any police officer who was a *real* cop knew that the jury got it wrong and felt sorry for the coward.

XII
THE MEETING

Immediately after the Valentine's Day massacre, Juan Perez, at the time the MDPD director, called MDPD's Tactical Unit training advisor, Lieutenant Joel Bello, and summoned him to the department's headquarters building.

Joel wasn't what one might have expected at first glance. He wasn't six feet tall, steroid-buffed, nor had the body of a weight lifter. He looked nothing like Rambo. Rather, he was more like Sergeant Elias from *Platoon*—highly disciplined, totally fearless, commanding respect by reputation for those who knew him, but more so for those who trained under him. He could have stepped straight out of that movie. The moment you saw him, you knew he was a real badass.

Every detail signaled experience: the precise military-style haircut, the taut, lean build, the precision gait, the way he carried himself. No nonsense. No bullshit. Focused. Poised. Street-smart. At five-foot-nine, his frame was lanky but sharply toned and visibly muscular. His jaw was chiseled, his eyes razor-sharp—coldly intelligent, exuding confidence and determination, an uncanny ability to accomplish the mission ordered.

Director Perez was different, but only in some ways. He had been a field officer, proud to wear the uniform and known for being a "straight-talker" whether liked or not. He was now management. Conversational, pleasant, mild-mannered, soft-spoken. If someone didn't know he ran one of the largest police departments in the country, they'd never even guess he was a cop. Although a political appointee, he still had quite a worthy background of distinctive service and was widely regarded as having the highest level of honesty and integrity. Beneath his gold accoutrements was a rock-solid cop at heart, and he led by example. He was decisive, laser-focused, and his occasional temper tantrum earned him the call sign "Lil General."

Joel respected him. Where Joel was raw, fast, field operations and street survival-driven, Perez was a measured administrator, calculating, the kind of man who could run an empire without ever raising his voice. In the chaos of a county on edge, Perez was the counterweight, the calm eye in the storm that brewed from the Parkland shooting.

Joel knew that while he could execute any mission with lethal precision, it was Perez who kept the whole MDPD machine from falling apart, such as what happened with BSO after the Parkland shooting only a few months earlier that year. They were the perfect match for the real, clear, and present likelihood of a repeat shooting in any Miami-Dade County public school.

Perez had the respect of MDPD's troops and the blessing of county politics, with quite a rare combination of the two in Miami-Dade. Since about 1960, the county had not elected a sheriff; the police director was a political mayoral appointment.

But Perez was nobody's puppet. He'd earned his appointment by his tenure, the hard way, climbing through the ranks through years of midnight calls, crime scenes, and internal storms. He was always fair, but also always firm. He had the mind of a strategist and the temperament of a diplomat. He was no longer a tactical man; he was the director.

When the door to the director's office closed, the complicated noise of police headquarters faded. The silence that followed was deliberate.

Perez lowered his voice, steady and controlled. "Joel, a year ago we talked about forming an emergency response team—something purpose-built for high-risk calls. At the time, we didn't have the personnel. And there was no appetite from the local offices to support it."

He let that settle.

"I need straight answers to two questions. But first—this morning the major called me in. He wanted to know exactly what we have in place to protect our school kids. I have the green light."

Joel held his gaze. "All right, Juan. Go ahead."

"Are our schools as vulnerable to a mass-casualty event like the one that just happened in Broward?"

Joel didn't blink; he was not surprised by the question. He met the director's gaze, steady and unflinching. "Yes."

Perez didn't react; he pretty much expected that response. He simply nodded up and down, slightly bowing his head. It was the answer he feared and now confirmed. "Second question. Do we have the training and resources, and can we retrain our patrol officers to handle it differently than BSO did?"

"No, sir."

Perez exhaled slowly, not in surprise—but in grim acknowledgment. "That's what I thought."

Joel's tense reply was quiet. "The big threat now is a copycat. These active-shooter incidents, even not in schools, per se, are occurring more frequently year after year. It's just a matter of time."

Perez leaned forward, the calm veneer giving way to urgency. "Here's what you do. Call or visit the major police departments in the country—LAPD, NYPD—and let's learn from their programs. Find out who's got the best active-shooter training program for a mass-casualty response. Time's not on our side. I don't want a repeat in Miami-Dade or to end up like BSO Sheriff Sergio Ismael. Find the best plan. Bring it here, and fast."

Sergio Ismael—the name hung heavy in the air. The Broward County sheriff when the Parkland shooting went down. Everyone knew the story. The fallout was brutal, public, and final. He was stripped of his badge and his post, a cautionary tale and wake-up call for Florida sheriffs.

No civil service rights for sheriffs. They served at the whim of the county mayor, but also the Florida governor. He went down fast; 2020 was an election year, and that didn't help the BSO sheriff either.

Joel broke the silence. "You can't be fired, only demoted. He was a sheriff. You're a police director."

"Ha." Perez gave a dry laugh. "Same shit. The shame's the same, and my last rank was captain, a major pay cut."

Joel met his eyes.

"My personal pride and economic interest aside, I could never live with myself if a kid got killed at one of our schools because we were unprepared," Perez said.

Joel needed no clarification. He understood. Perez was visceral in his text, and his tone was clear—time was of the essence.

Joel had his marching orders. "Yes, sir."

He walked out of the director's office, carrying more than just orders, but the weight of prevention—of duty to school kids.

If another massacre unfolded on his watch, it wouldn't just be a professional failure; it would be personal. The headlines would fade, but the memory and guilt wouldn't; no redemption, no legacy—only the memory of lives he couldn't save. That was never going to happen. The clock was ticking.

He needed to set up an active-shooter program that was actually proven to work practically in the current world, then recruitment, and then training. The mission launched the instant Joel stepped out of the director's office. This would all be fast-tracked.

In Joel's head, the job was like a 911 call he'd already answered the moment Perez closed the door and sent him on this mission. He moved like a man who understood the math of the risk and the dates on the calendar. If this were the summer, he'd have more time, but school was still in session. He also knew what he was looking for. There were only two viable responses to these volatile, fast-moving active-shooter threats.

One, swiftly approach and take out the threat. Two, slow everything down; surround it, control a perimeter, negotiate, buy time—let the scene play out while you manage risk to bystanders. Both had potentially bad consequences.

But Joel's instincts pointed him in only one direction. But could modern society and civil liability expense tolerate that approach? He knew that decades ago, the hold-wait-and-see approach worked, but times had changed.

Before exiting headquarters, Joel called his travel agent and arranged his itinerary. He gave himself just enough time to go home, pack a suitcase, and head to the airport, making calls and setting appointments with the various police department training coordinators on the way. By wheels-up time, about two hours later, everything was in place.

He hadn't stopped since Perez gave him his orders. The mission would consume him: Sleep came in fragments—two, maybe three hours at a time—time zones blurred with the cross-country flights. Meals came in bites, but they usually were an afterthought. Personal plans, routine appointments, family time—everything else canceled.

Joel's research and visits revealed a general consensus that neither option was perfect. But the data didn't lie, and neither did Joel's instincts. The choice was obvious. He adopted the Hercules Program, a model developed by the New York Police Department that embraced the second, much bolder, approach: rapid identification, immediate movement, decisive action. It was built on one principle: End the threat before it multiplied.

Joel landed at Miami International Airport and went straight to headquarters—no time to rest, no need for small talk. His due diligence was done; he *had* the plan. He had traveled nearly 10,000 miles, department after department, shaking every relevant hand and gathering every piece of intelligence he needed on active-shooter and mass-casualty attack policies.

Sitting across from Perez again, Joel's eyes carried the burden and results of the task now accomplished.

Director Perez wasn't surprised to hear from Joel so soon. He was visibly anxious. Was it going to be a status update, a rough draft, or the final plan? He should've known better.

The moment Joel walked into the office, Perez saw exhaustion written all over him—dark circles, hollow eyes, the kind of fatigue that comes from running on adrenaline and fast food for days. Still, his posture was steady, his stride deliberate.

"Joel, you look like shit," Perez said flatly.

Joel cracked a grin. "Yep, I know! I feel like it, too. My wife picked me up an hour ago and said the same thing. I have what you asked for."

He carefully set a new, neatly configured, and tabbed binder on the director's desk. The title on the front page read *Miami-Dade Police Department's Mass Casualty and Active Shooter Response Policy*.

"This," Joel said, his tone firm but respectful, "is the written plan and policy I recommend, the ink still fresh, so to speak."

"Hold my calls and lower my police communication radio," Director Perez barked at his secretary. He opened the binder and read it carefully, focusing with the turn of every page. The room went still—there was no phone ringing, no radio chatter bleeding through the walls—just the quiet breeze of the air conditioner and the soft sound of paper turning.

When he finally looked up, there was something different in his eyes—surprise, but not disbelief.

"What's the matter?" Joel asked.

Perez exhaled slowly. "It's...aggressive—very aggressive. But I'm not surprised. Some will argue that this goes against everything in the book—contain and control. But if NYPD uses it, we will, too."

"Yes, sir," Joel said, steady. "There is no control with a crazed, active shooter if you don't stop it. It's the best, if not the *only*, way. We need to change the policy and tactical response—direct, immediate, and elimination.

"The folks behind Hercules have the most historical research and the stats—I saw them," Joel went on, voice steady. "The greater chance of stopping the killing is a fast, direct, decisive response—even if the officer who gets there first is alone. You don't wait for backup. It's dangerous as hell, but it's effective, as it's more dangerous for the victims or other civilians who are nearby. I saw the numbers."

Perez studied him for a long beat, the weight of the claim settling between them. He tapped the binder once, slow. "Okay, Hercules it is."

Joel shook his head. "Let's rename it."

Perez leaned back, still processing. "Okay," he said after a pause. "Let's run it by legal. If they clear it, then we'll talk about implementation."

"I already did," Joel replied, sliding another binder forward. "Here it is. It's all the case law and court opinions."

Perez let out a quiet, almost resigned laugh. "Why am I not surprised?" He nodded. "So, let's get SRT on this right away."

SRT, the Special Response Team, was the highly trained law enforcement unit tasked with handling the highest-risk incidents that ordinary patrol officers weren't equipped for.

Joel shook his head. "SRT isn't the right fit for this, sir."

Director Perez looked up from the document, his expression tightening. "Why not?"

Joel hesitated for a moment. He knew better than to challenge the chain of command, but behind closed doors, between the two of them, formality had its limits.

"Juan," he said carefully, "those SRT guys are great—rappelling of ropes on building balconies and roofs, breaching doors, sniping, hostage negotiations, all of it. But they're not built for *this* kind of plan."

Perez listened, silent, eyes fixed intently on Joel.

"They've developed certain training and habits inconsistent with applying Hercules to what happened at Parkland; they have different instincts, tactics, and strategies," Joel continued. "What we're facing here with an active-shooter/mass-attack casualty is *different*. It's total chaos—mass death and injury in real time. This Hercules policy is quite different. You can't just regear SRT's mentality."

Perez leaned back slightly. "I agree. This is definitely not for SRT?"

"Correct, sir. Look, they mainly respond well after the fact to situations already contained, separated, and controlled, and then they negotiate. That's not an active-shooter or mass-attack casualty scenario. This Hercules Program is about the officers responding immediately to the scene—moving in, fast, deliberate, neutralizing the threat before it grows. That's not SRT's world, Juan. It has to be *mentally different*."

"So, you're saying we run this through Uniform Patrol Division? Joel, that'll take months—"

Joel cut Perez off before he could finish. "No, sir. This has to be now. Let's uncage Sergeant Manny Malgor. He will train and run a highly selective, specialized unit pulled from Uniform Patrol."

"So...what's next?" asked Perez, leaning forward slightly, his tone curious but measured.

"It's in the policy I handed you, sir," Joel replied. He paused, allowing himself a faint half-smile as he looked down at the floor, choosing his words carefully. He knew his boundaries—but he also knew straightforward honesty was part of the job.

"I'm so glad you're in charge of training. You remember, I'm the one who put you there, right? Not because of our friendship, Joel—but because you were the top choice. The next candidate wasn't even close. You never fail, Joel. You never disappoint, but let's let Manny run it operationally."

"I agree with you, Juan," Joel said.

Perez leaned back, lowering his voice. "There were a lot of applicants for that position. And that's exactly why I called you after Parkland, and why we're sitting here now. You've got the mind and the heart for this. You should keep seeking promotions."

Manny nodded respectfully. "I appreciate that, Juan. But I'm happy where I am right now, running the Training Bureau. You know what happens if I get promoted to captain—I go back to road patrol like every rookie sergeant. No special favors." He gave a faint grin. "And truth be told, I'd miss running that unit."

"Now tell me," Perez said, leaning forward, elbows on the desk, how soon? And should I call it Hercules?"

Joel shook his head immediately. "Hell no! I already thought about that on my flight back to Miami. It's simple—and it defines the mission. Priority Response Team. PRT."

Perez nodded slowly, the name rolling off his tongue. "PRT...I had thought of ERT [Emergency Response Team], but I like PRT."

Joel reached into his folder and slid a single-page chart across the desk. "Here's the flow chart. I've geographically divided the county into nine equivalent regions—one PRT team per area. Rotating shifts for full twenty-four-hour coverage. Each squad led by one sergeant, and I want—"

Perez cut him off. "You mean *we* want..."

"Yes, Juan," Joel said, with quiet conviction. "*We* want no rookies and no veterans. Two to four years' experience—enough to know the streets, but no bad habits yet. Fit, fast, fearless. Preferably single, no kids—nothing to make them hesitate when it's time to move."

Perez gave a dry, knowing smirk. "You know how this'll play if an innocent civilian is injured or killed by a PRT use of force, right? The complaints, the optics..."

"I don't give a shit if he, she, or *they all* complain," Joel cut in. "This is about saving lives, Juan."

Perez looked at him across the desk—saw the conviction in his eyes and the weight of a man who knew exactly what was at stake. "Didn't a US president once say you can satisfy some people some of the time, but not all people all the time?" the director asked. He continued, "Something like that...and it was Lincoln or Washington, maybe Kennedy."

"It was Lincoln, sir," Joel replied.

"You sure?" Perez asked.

"Yep," said Joel.

Perez shook his head. "I took history in high school... Let's check Google real quick... Holy shit, Joel, it *was* Lincoln."

Joel laughed. "What high school did you go to, Juan?"

Perez threw up his hands, still chuckling. "Fuck you, Joel. Get out of here. I'll brief the mayor—she's waiting for me. This is her *top* priority."

"Did you say *priority*, sir?"

"You heard right."

They chuckled together. Joel paused and finally said, "Priority Response Team. We will be operational in thirty days. And Juan, we ain't changing that name. Screw whatever name the mayor wants—this is *your* creation."

Perez smiled, looked down at the floor, then back at Joel. "*Ours*," he said.

Perez exhaled through his nose, rubbing his temples. "I'll check with Legal—see if we can do it without some asshole lawyer suing us under the ADA."

"Sir..." Joel paused. "Legal approved that, too."

"Jesus Christ, Joel...did you?" Perez asked, eyebrows raised.

"Yep, that box is already checked off," Joel replied calmly. "It's not a violation of Title VII if we call it *operational necessity*. It has been bulletproof tested in court."

Perez rubbed a hand across his jaw, the tension clear in his face.

Joel continued, firm and deliberate. "Obviously, we cannot—and *will not*—include or exclude any applicant based on age, sex, race, or nationality. And we'll strive for a diverse cross-section. But we will have high training and fitness standards, and whoever doesn't pass...doesn't pass."

"Would you like me to join the meeting in case the mayor has any questions?" Joel asked.

"She may not," Perez replied. "You have a very detailed policy here, Joel."

Joel returned a warm smile, then paused, measuring his words. "Juan, remember this—you are the politician, I'm the tactician."

Perez leaned back, a smirk tugging his lips. "Listen to yourself... There *is* some politician in you, Joel. You might want to reconsider a new career path."

Joel shook his head. "Doubtful, sir. It's just not in my chip—not my DNA."

Both officers stood and shook hands. "I don't need to tell you this, but thanks," Perez said, his voice steady. "Job well done and at lightning speed."

Joel shook his head. "Sir, tell the mayor this was *your* plan; it really was. I just put the pieces together. I'm not a politician—don't need the credit. What only matters to me is that this is the best way—the only way—to best protect our citizens...and more importantly, our kids."

Perez replied, "If an active shooter gets into any of our schools, we have a better chance to save many lives with PRT—that we'd otherwise more likely lose."

"Unfortunately, the only way we'll ever know for sure," Joel said, "is if another mass-casualty attack or active shooter happens. And let's hope that day never comes. The high visibility of school resource officers is still and always will be a good deterrent."

"You're right on that, Joel. Let's hope it's never tested," Perez said quietly.

At the threshold of the door, with one hand on the knob, Joel stopped. "Sir, weeks ago, you asked me if we were ready. We were not; we still aren't, but within the next few weeks, I promise you that I'll have the unit selected and preliminary trained.

"Juan, anybody you want to put in PRT?"

"Nope, you pick them. No influence; pick only the best qualified."

He straightened his shoulders, gave Perez a final nod, and opened the door. As he walked out and closed it firmly behind him, the soft thud of the latch seemed to punctuate the weight of their conversation.

Before reaching his car in the headquarters parking lot, Joel pulled out his phone and dictated a countywide email announcing open positions for PRT applicants.

By the time he reached his vehicle, some notifications were already coming in—officers replying, asking questions, expressing interest. The momentum was clear. He started the engine, the low rumble a quiet reminder that the real work—selection, training, and readiness—was only just beginning.

Within a few more minutes and throughout the following days, Joel's email inbox was inundated with applicants. Some he knew well, others only marginally, and a few not at all.

He pulled the human resources and internal affairs files on each aspirant, scrutinizing their records, experience, temperament, fitness, and performance evaluations. Methodically, he weeded out those who wouldn't meet the strict criteria.

Within a week, about 100 interviews took place, all selections were made, and the logistics for personnel transfers were finalized. The personnel for the PRT were now in place.

Manny scheduled a meeting at MDPD's Training Bureau for all PRT selectees. A few PowerPoint slides were enough to outline the PRT's mission. The same marked patrol units already assigned would be used, only adding decals identifying them as PRT. Training would begin immediately, and there was no time for delay.

The PRT training began immediately at the state of the MDPD's Training Bureau. It consisted of practicums, intense shooting scenarios, firearms selections, quick reloading skills, reviews and testing of the new written policy, and first responder training in trauma and triage settings. Every practice was designed based on prior active-shooter incidents, giving officers the chance to react in conditions as close to reality as possible.

Everyone understood that no two incidents would ever be identical. The focus was clear: rapid identification of the threat, decisive neutralization, and then immediate transition to Phase 2—the medical emergency response of "gear and go."

PRT formally went into action a few months later. Even after this initial training, in-service training continued very regularly to keep the PRT officers' skills sharp. The program and policy weren't complex—it was about precision and consistency. Every week, the team drilled, reinforced communications, and refined coordination. Members were required to know the mission and the memorial. The nearest squad would move first, with additional units joining as the situation demanded.

When PRT finally rolled out, every detail mattered. Every second counted. And somewhere in the back of Joel's mind, he knew that despite all the planning, the real test and final results—when the alarms finally sounded—would be entirely unpredictable.

XIII
THE TAKEDOWN

5:31 p.m.

"Fuel alert's on." Mateo's voice tightened. "We got maybe five to ten minutes at this pace."

"We're real close," Mateo said, scanning the mirrors. "Jesus—I've never seen so many units. Only time I saw this many was at an officer's funeral."

"Don't say that," Lindner shot back. "Get the lead. Looks like Mirabal and Santiesteban are still right behind it."

"One hundred percent," Mateo agreed.

"Fuck, there's a ton of civilian traffic," Lindner warned.

"Translate that—a lot of potential civilian casualties. They could take out thirty, easy. That's Parkland numbers," Mateo said, quiet and hard.

"That's not happening again, brother," Lindner said.

"I'm with you," Mateo replied.

"The hostage—he's as good as dead," Mateo said after a long beat. "Poor soul. Pray he stays down. They're not letting him go; if they were going to use him to negotiate, they already would've done that."

"No shit, Sherlock," Lindner muttered.

"Fuck," Lindner said.

"Keep going. They gotta be on fumes, too," Lindner added.

"Look—there it is. They're slowing to a stop. That's our chance," Mateo said.

"The threat's from both sides. We need a modified *L*—think short *U*. Cut the crossfire and stop them from using the hostage as a human shield."

"Exactly," Lindner said. "Short *U*. Keep it tight."

The radio hummed. Tires whispered on asphalt. Ahead, the UPS truck crawled to a near-full stop—a pause pregnant with danger. The brake lights flared red. Instead of taking the obvious escape route around the cluster of civilian cars, the driver steered deliberately into the pocket of traffic and settled there, boxed in. A calculated move. With so many bystanders nearby, they assumed no office would risk an escalation.

They figured right, but also wrong. Had they opened the door, released the hostage, and tossed out the weapons, the standoff would have snapped shut right then and there.

Every cop in the convoy leaned into their training, into the plan. Seconds, not minutes, would decide how many lives walked away.

Then the truck's brake lights flared red.

The vehicle slowed, heavy and deliberate, before coming to a complete halt in the middle of the roadway. No sudden swerves. No last-second acceleration. This was either a surrender or a shoot-out.

Dozens of officers advanced in a classic C-formation, the arc tightened around the truck, and every firearm was pointed at the truck.

Commands rang out, sharp and unmistakable, cutting through the heavy air.

There was movement. It looked like the driver was getting up from his seat.

XIV
THE SPOTLIGHT

For over thirty years after leaving the MDPD, Rick had worn many hats—one as a lawyer, another as an invited speaker at various local and international law schools, and as the voice the media trusted when police work turned violent. He'd become a regular on local and international broadcasts, the "go-to guy" newsrooms called when the footage was raw, and the facts were unclear.

On December 5, 2019, the morning the news broke, his phone lit up. Telemundo. Univision. Channel 6. Channel 10. Everyone wanted his take. In-person and Zoom interviews stacked one after another.

This was major news—national coverage. After Parkland, it was among the biggest active-shooter cases in the country of the era.

He reviewed the cell phone and helicopter footage carefully. He slowed the video, studying it frame by frame, then watched it in reverse before running it again at normal speed several times. Within minutes, he felt confident in what he was seeing.

To Rick, the shooting was justified. The officers had

responded exactly as they had been trained to. He said as much publicly. In his view, every officer involved would be cleared—within the year, and likely sooner.

The backlash came fast and furious. Friends, colleagues, even a few former officers—most hadn't watched the full video, and some hadn't seen it at all. They didn't understand the chaos of that moment or the split-second choices that defined survival. Rick did—he'd been there forty years earlier, and he stood by his opinion.

Indeed, the Broward SAO had just indicted Scot Anderson for doing the opposite—standing back while people died at Marjory Stoneman Douglas.

These officers pushed forward, toward the threat, without shields and with minimal cover, facing two heavily armed robbers who had no intention of surrendering. They had stopped the killing; they were trying to stop the bleeding. They had done what Anderson didn't have the courage to do. And because of that, Rick believed they would be all right.

Five years later...

"Hey, Rick. Tony Pipitone, NBC Channel 6. You hear about the robbery, the UPS truck hijack, and the police shooting?"

"Yes, sir."

"With your police and criminal defense background, can we interview you for your input?"

"Of course. As I said years ago, it was a good shooting, from the little I know," Rick chirped.

"That's what we want, again, your analysis. Why—"

Rick interrupted. "Tony, I can do this micro or macro. I can give you one single reason or ten."

"Rick, didn't you hear? They're indicting four MDPD officers in that case."

Rick cut him off. "What? Impossible. That was five years ago. That's a bullshit political move. Plain wrong. Jesus Christ...poor guys."

Tony hung up, but the conversation lingered in Rick's mind, replaying alongside everything else he'd heard that morning. Before he could process it fully, his phone lit up again.

Rick's sister was calling.

"You heard?" he asked when he picked up.

"Yup."

"He's got a PBA lawyer."

There was a pause.

"And?"

"The one they assigned is the brother-in-law of the PBA president."

Another pause.

"No surprise there. He's a good lawyer."

In the aftermath of the shooting, the decision buzzed with speculation and criticism, the kind that could eat at an officer's sleep. Four separate shooting incidents had unfolded in quick succession: the jewelry store in Miami-Dade County, one on the Turnpike, another on I-75, and the final, chaotic scene at Flamingo Road and Miramar Parkway. The jewelry store itself never recovered from the ordeal, eventually closing and reopening over on the beach.

The Turnpike shooting was not so defined. It wasn't clear whether the suspect had fired at Sergeant Machado, and even *if* he had, it became irrelevant once he was killed.

The officer's own discharge of her weapon wasn't an issue; no one inside the UPS truck had been hit.

By any measure, it was a *clean shooting*. Critics could have argued she shouldn't have put herself in a moving-vehicle gunfight, but under the circumstances, no one said it. She was cleared—good to go. No casings, no stray bullets—nothing left behind to question.

The third shooting was straightforward: The UPS truck driver fired four rounds at a moving marked police unit. Three of those rounds were traceable to the firearms recovered from the suspects, leaving little ambiguity about what had happened. Another clean shooting.

The fourth scene, however, was an entirely different beast. Over 200 rounds were fired, and there was blood everywhere. It was chaotic, dangerous, and almost impossible to preserve; it had been contaminated by too many bullets, too many casings, and *too* many people—officers and civilians alike. Two civilian victims survived the initial exchange, but one later died at a nearby hospital. The third and fourth victims—the robbers—were pronounced dead at the scene.

Assigning responsibility for the investigation became a bureaucratic chess match. Multiple agencies were involved—Miami-Dade, the FBI, FDLE, and the Broward County Sheriff's Office.

What baffled the shooting officers and their PBA attorneys was the prolonged silence stretching from the summer of 2021 through mid-2024. There was nothing left to discover. The Broward County State Attorney's Office had already secured every report, every sworn statement, every shell casing, ballistic, and medical examiner's report. At that point, the investigative pursuit no longer appeared rooted in fact-finding.

Rumor had it that after the deceased civilians' attorneys

lost their federal civil rights lawsuit, they pivoted aggressively—allegedly lobbying for criminal charges against the officers involved. Maybe that was true. Maybe it wasn't. But the timing made the situation feel unmistakably political.

By June 2021, FDLE had formally closed its investigation. The agency did not make charging decisions; it compiled findings and forwarded them to the appropriate jurisdictional prosecutor for review. Its role was procedural, not prosecutorial.

It became clear that the SAO wasn't examining the robbers' actions, but rather the officers'—not the decision to open fire on armed suspects, but whether the return fire—those seconds of chaos—had somehow crossed a legal line. The working theory was manslaughter: that the officers' bullets, fired in defense of life, had "transferred" to the two innocent civilians and caused their deaths.

It was a hollow, technical argument. The kind that ignored the noise, the blood, and the impossible split-second choices made in real time. But the case had pressure behind it—families demanding answers, civil lawyers circling, headlines waiting. Someone had to carry the blame, and the dead couldn't.

The tragedy was that the law already accounted for this kind of moment. Since 1922, Florida had recognized transferred intent—that if someone used lawful force in self-defense or to protect another, and an innocent person was unintentionally hurt, no crime was committed. Later, the state expanded that principle under its stand-your-ground statute, granting pretrial immunity to anyone, including police officers, whose use of force was objectively reasonable to prevent death or great harm.

But when the Broward State Attorney convened the Broward Grand Jury, that law was never mentioned. No explanation. No reference. Just the raw facts stripped of their legal context.

Whether it was an oversight or a choice, no one could say for sure. But to those who'd been there that day, it felt like the same story told too many times before—men who ran toward danger now standing alone in its aftermath.

The prosecutor's theory of liability was fundamentally unfair. It blatantly ignored the ballistics evidence and the medical examiner's conclusions regarding the two robbers.

The state relied almost exclusively on civilian eyewitness testimony from individuals who witnessed the shooting. Further, investigators matched bullets recovered from the deceased civilians to the issued firearms of specific officers and built the case around those matches alone.

Only those officers were arrested.

In the summer of 2024, a grand jury was impaneled in Broward County, Florida. The case was assigned to one of the county's most seasoned prosecutors—Assistant State Attorney Calvin Monroe.

Monroe had spent nearly fifty years in the trenches. He'd tried it all—rape, robbery, murder, drug trafficking—the full spectrum of violent and high-profile crime. A longtime adjunct law school professor, Monroe was a fixture in the courthouse. Judges, defense attorneys, and prosecutors alike knew him well.

He was quiet but unyielding—sharp, methodical, and disarmingly calm. Even in his late seventies, age had only tempered him, not weakened him. Standing six-foot-two and weighing around 250 pounds, he carried the kind of presence that filled a courtroom without effort.

Soft-spoken and deliberate, Monroe's voice carried more weight than volume. His reputation was that of a man who never lost control—one who could bend a case his way through patience, precision, and the quiet certainty that came from decades of watching justice unfold, however imperfectly. He was a legendary prosecutor and an excellent advocate. Now older, hard of hearing, slow, and disoriented, he still had the savvy of a true, battle-tested veteran.

Four MDPD officers were indicted. One denied having fired his weapon when, in fact, he had. No one knew why he said it. Maybe fear. Maybe confusion. Or maybe the dawning realization that, in this new climate, the truth could ruin a career faster than a bullet could end a life.

The media coverage was relentless. Every headline carried a hint of accusation, every photo framed for outrage. The officers' faces were splashed across screens and front pages as if guilt were already established. In living rooms across South Florida, people formed opinions before the evidence ever reached the courtroom. What had begun as a moment of heroism, a desperate effort to stop violent men, had turned into a public spectacle.

All officers were suspended without pay.

By protocol, any officer who discharged their firearm could not be compelled to give a statement that might later be used by the State Attorney's Office in determining criminal liability or at a subsequent trial. It didn't make much difference in this case. FDLE had access to body-worn camera footage from every officer on scene. They could see what each one said, where they were positioned, how they moved, and when they fired.

Rick's phone rang. It was his sister again.

"Rick, I need you to represent him—or at least meet with him. Tell him what you think. Just meet him, please," his sister said. "Did you hear?" she added, breathless.

"Hear what?"

"The State Attorney's Office in Broward just announced it. They're charging the four officers with manslaughter."

Rick froze. "Get out."

"I'm serious."

Silence.

He stared at the wall, the line still open, his sister's voice fading into background noise. The weight of the conversation lingered long after the call ended, settling into something heavier—unavoidable.

The next morning, Officer Jose Mateo arrived alone at Rick's office. After the usual exchange of pleasantries, Mateo leaned forward and said, "Oscar says you're the best. That's why I'm here. I need to know."

"Jose, a case like this will cost between $1 and $2 million in billable time," Rick said plainly. "You're suspended without pay. The PBA isn't going to fund me, especially if it means I'm effectively going against the president's brother-in-law. So, tell me, how are you staying afloat?"

"My squad's been covering me," Jose said quietly.

Rick sat back, studying him. He was genuinely surprised. Loyalty like that wasn't common—not when careers and families were on the line. He paused, weighing on what he needed to see, what would justify committing to Jose and stepping into something this massive.

"I can't handle this as a multi-defendant case," Rick finally said. "It would take thousands of hours and at least two years to get to trial. There would be close to 200 witnesses to depose. A good expert will cost about $100,000."

He leaned forward. "I'll take your case. But you separate from the pack. I choose no more than ten critical depositions. We move fast. We move alone."

"This case is 75 percent a stand-your-ground fight," he said. "And I'm going to push it hard, because I'm confident this was a justified shooting. If we win at that stage, there's no jury trial."

He let that sit for a moment.

"If we lose, we demand a speedy trial, and we go in fast and aggressive."

Rick's eyes stayed fixed on Jose. "But we only do this if you break away from the others. No codefendants. No group strategy. Just you and me, moving fast and staying focused."

He paused. "Are you okay with that?"

Jose nodded once. "Whatever you say, Rick. I trust you."

"Good," Rick said.

They stood and shook hands, sealing the decision. Outside, the world was still waiting for answers, but inside that office, a path had been chosen.

From this point forward, everything would change.

ACKNOWLEDGMENTS

I would like to recognize the following individuals for their professional, creative, and emotional support in the preparation of this publication: my wife, Annie; my daughter, Nikki; my son, Ricki; and my assistant, Julianne.

I also extend my deepest appreciation to the following officers for their dedicated service to our community, and in supporting Mateo during our courtroom battle: Oscar Ordiales; Jarvys Duran; Dimitri Gardner; Ricardo Benavides; Hector Monegro; Daritza Machado; Edward Quintana; Shereyra Rubio; Bradley Gomez; Stephen McGuire; Danny Fernandez; Sgt. Norberto Gonzalez II; Sgt. Jacob Lendic; Sgt. Oliver Mayorga; and Sgt. Safiuddin Mohammed.

www.ingramcontent.com/pod-product-compliance
Lightning Source LLC
LaVergne TN
LVHW100354240926
848801LV00016B/178/J